Reading & Writing
Ha Long Bay

NATIONAL
GEOGRAPHIC
L E A R N I N G

Australia • Brazil • Mexico • Singapore • United Kingdom • United States

National Geographic Learning,
a Cengage Company

Reading & Writing, Ha Long Bay

**Lauri Blass, Mari Vargo, Keith S. Folse,
April Muchmore-Vokoun, Elena Vestri**

Publisher: Sherrise Roehr

Executive Editor: Laura LeDréan

Managing Editor: Jennifer Monaghan

Digital Implementation Manager,
Irene Boixareu

Senior Media Researcher: Leila Hishmeh

Director of Global Marketing: Ian Martin

Regional Sales and National Account
Manager: Andrew O'Shea

Content Project Manager: Ruth Moore

Senior Designer: Lisa Trager

Manufacturing Planner: Mary Beth
Hennebury

Composition: Lumina Datamatics

For permission to use material from this text or product,
submit all requests online at **cengage.com/permissions**
Further permissions questions can be emailed to
permissionrequest@cengage.com

Student Edition: Reading & Writing, Ha Long Bay
ISBN-13: 978-0-357-13834-2

National Geographic Learning
20 Channel Center Street
Boston, MA 02210
USA

Locate your local office at **international.cengage.com/region**

Visit National Geographic Learning online at **ELTNGL.com**
Visit our corporate website at **www.cengage.com**

Printed in China
Print Number: 02   Print Year: 2019

PHOTO CREDITS

Scope and Sequence

SOCIAL RELATIONSHIPS

Polar bear cubs stay with their
mothers for more than two years.

THINK AND DISCUSS

1 Aside from humans, what other animals live
in social groups?
2 What similarities do you think there are between
human relationships and animal relationships?

A Read the information on these pages and answer the questions.

1. What are some examples of nonhuman primates?

2. What similarities have researchers discovered between humans and other primates?

B Match the words in blue to their definitions.

_____ (v) to behave toward someone in a particular way

_____ (v) to communicate with someone or something

_____ (v) to look after someone (usually a young, sick, or old person)

Families of wild macaques often bathe in the hot springs in Yamanouchi, Japan.

SOCIAL ANIMALS

Researchers have discovered that humans share certain behavioral characteristics with other primates—the group of mammals that includes humans, monkeys, and apes.

Basic Communication

Primatologists—scientists who study primates—have found that some apes are capable of basic communication using human sign language. Researchers have also observed apes inventing and using tools to get food and complete other tasks.

Social Behavior

Both humans and other primates tend to live in social groups, and they share some characteristics in terms of their social behavior. Researchers today are looking at the similarities and differences in how humans and animals interact within their own social groups, for example, how they treat each other and care for their young.

Reading 1

PREPARING TO READ

BUILDING
VOCABULARY

A The words in blue below are used in Reading 1. Read the paragraph. Then match the correct form of each word to its definition.

Most workplaces are positive environments where people work well together. However, an **aggressive** employee in an office can easily lead to workplace stress—by treating coworkers unfairly, **criticizing** them, or taking credit for their work. Employees who experience workplace **conflict** on a regular basis can lose **motivation** to do good work. Why do some employees not cooperate with their coworkers? It may be that the employee is **ambitious** and thinks that aggressive **behavior** will help them get ahead. Or the employee is afraid of losing **status** in the company and thinks that aggressive behavior will help them stay on top.

1. _____ (n) a serious disagreement

2. _____ (n) the way someone acts

3. _____ (adj) acting in a forceful or competitive way

4. _____ (n) a feeling of being excited to do something

5. _____ (v) to speak badly of someone or something

6. _____ (adj) wanting to be successful

7. _____ (n) an individual's position within a group

USING
VOCABULARY

B Discuss these questions with a partner.

1. How **ambitious** are you? Would you rather be a president of a company, or a low-level or mid-level employee without a lot of responsibilities? Why?

2. How would you react to an **aggressive** coworker? Give an example.

BRAINSTORMING

C Discuss your answers to these questions in groups.

1. In what ways do you think employees cooperate in the workplace? Give two examples.

2. In what ways do you think primates cooperate in the wild? Give two examples.

PREDICTING

D Read the title, headings, and captions in the reading passage. How do you think human behavior in the office is similar to primate behavior in the jungle? Write three ideas. Then check your ideas as you read.

_____

_____

_____

THE APE
IN THE OFFICE

🎧 Track 1

A   Does the "office jungle" mirror behavior in the real jungle? New research shows people in offices may use conflict and cooperation in similar ways to primates in the jungle.

B   Animal behavior specialist Richard Conniff is the author of *The Ape in the Corner Office*. In his book, Conniff examines corporate behavior through the eyes of a primatologist. He suggests cooperation is the key to success for both humans and other primates. He sees similarities in the ways they use social networks and hierarchies[1] to gain status. He also points out that while conflict can be effective at times, both humans and apes usually prefer to cooperate.

[1] **Hierarchies** are groups or situations that are organized from higher to lower by rank, social status, or function.

COOPERATION VERSUS CONFLICT

C

People often think that the animal world is full of conflict. However, conflict and aggression actually play a smaller role in the wild than cooperation. In fact, according to Conniff, both humans and other primates are social creatures, and both groups normally try to avoid conflict. Chimpanzees, for example, typically spend their days caring for their young and traveling together in small groups. Conniff points out that chimps spend about 5 percent of the day being aggressive, but 15 to 20 percent of the day grooming[2] each other. For humans and other primates, conflict is rare and does not last long. For both species, cooperation is a more effective way to succeed and survive.

THE VALUE OF NETWORKING

D

Research also shows that people and other primates use similar social networking strategies to get ahead in life. They create tight social bonds by sharing resources, doing each other favors, building teams, and making friends. Employees with ambitious career goals, for example, often rely on powerful people in their office to help them get better jobs. In a similar way, chimps work to strengthen relationships with other chimps.

E

Frans de Waal, a primatologist at Emory University in Atlanta, Georgia, claims that for chimps, "you can never reach a high position in their world if you don't have friends who help you." In fact, research shows that chimps often create bonds to strengthen their status, or importance, in the community. They do favors for one another and share resources. They sometimes also use their cunning[3] to get ahead. "In chimps a common strategy is to break up alliances that can be used against them," de Waal explains. "They see a main rival sitting with someone else and they try to break up [that meeting]."

▽ Aggressive behavior may bring results, but also leads to isolation for the aggressor.

[2] Grooming is the activity of animals cleaning each other.
[3] Cunning is the ability to achieve things in a clever way, often by deceiving other people.

▲ Chest-pounding is a sign of aggression among gorillas.

THE IMPORTANCE OF HIERARCHIES

F Groups of coworkers and primate groups have similar social rules. In both cases, the groups organize themselves into hierarchies, and individual members know their roles. Individuals in both human and ape groups have a particular position in relation to other group members. This decides their behavior in the group. For example, young people may speak softly or avoid eye contact when they talk to people with higher status. Similarly, Conniff explains that when chimpanzees approach a powerful or senior member, they try to make themselves look as small as they can.

THE LIMITS OF AGGRESSION

G Although cooperation is more common in groups, both humans and other primates sometimes use conflict in order to gain status. Aggressive behaviors get attention, and they show an individual's power in the group. People sometimes shout or intimidate others to make a point or win an argument. Apes show aggression by pounding their chests, screeching, or hitting trees. However, Conniff notes that conflict does not gain long-term success for either species. When bosses criticize their employees, treat them unfairly, or make their working lives difficult, employees become stressed, lose motivation, and quit their jobs. When apes are aggressive, they chase other apes away. In both cases, aggressive individuals can become isolated, and neither humans nor apes want to be alone.

H In his book, Conniff makes the case that interacting in a kind and polite way is more beneficial for both humans and primates. "The truth is we are completely dependent on other people emotionally as well as for our physical needs," Conniff concludes. "We function as part of a group rather than as individuals." Employees who cooperate in the office and primates who cooperate in the wild find themselves happier, more effective, and more likely to survive.

UNDERSTANDING THE READING

UNDERSTANDING
PURPOSE

A According to the reading passage, what were the two main reasons Conniff wrote *The Ape in the Corner Office*? Check (✓) the most suitable answers.

☐ 1. to explain how apes and humans behave similarly

☐ 2. to show how humans have learned from animal behavior

☐ 3. to argue that animals cooperate better than humans do

☐ 4. to show how humans and other primates value cooperation

SUMMARIZING

B Complete the summary below. Write no more than one word in each space.

People in offices and primates in the wild both prefer to [1] _____ with one another and avoid [2] _____ . They also use social [3] _____ skills to be successful. Both groups organize themselves into [4] _____ , which affect how they behave in a group. While uncommon, both office workers and primates sometimes use [5] _____ behavior to assert themselves.

CATEGORIZING

C Complete the Venn diagram with examples (a–j) from the reading passage describing human and other primate behavior.

a. speak softly or avoid eye contact
b. share resources
c. do favors
d. build teams
e. groom one another

f. travel together in groups
g. do well in groups
h. pound chests, screech, or hit trees
i. rely on powerful people to get better jobs
j. reduce body size to look smaller

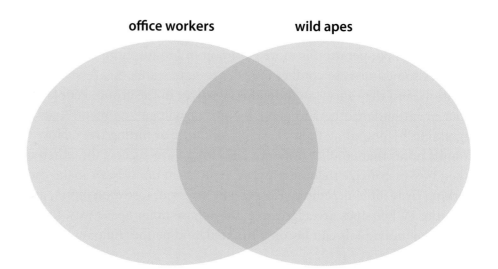

office workers   **wild apes**

CRITICAL THINKING When a writer is making a claim or an argument, it is important to **analyze the evidence** (examples, statistics, research, etc.) that they provide. As you read, think about and evaluate the evidence mentioned. Does this evidence clearly support the writer's main ideas?

D What evidence does the writer use in the passage to support their main idea in each section? Complete the chart with the key points of evidence.

Section	Evidence
Cooperation versus Conflict	Statistics:
The Value of Networking	An expert / Research:
The Importance of Hierarchies	An example:
The Limits of Aggression	An example:

E Work in groups. Look at the evidence in exercise D. Based on the evidence provided, which section do you think is the least convincing? Why?

F Find and underline the following words in the reading. Use context to identify their meanings. Then circle the correct options to complete the definitions.

> bonds (paragraph D) intimidate (paragraph G)
> rival (paragraph E) beneficial (paragraph H)

1. If an interaction is *beneficial*, it is **useless / useful**.

2. A *rival* is someone you are **cooperating / competing** with.

3. If you *intimidate* people, you make them feel **frightened / happy** enough to do what you want them to do.

4. If you have strong *bonds* with someone, you feel very **connected to / distant from** them.

G Work with a partner. Can you think of two examples from your own experience that either support or contradict the ideas expressed in the reading?

_____

_____

DEVELOPING READING SKILLS

READING SKILL Identifying Main and Supporting Ideas

The main idea of a paragraph is the most important idea, or the idea that the paragraph is about. It is often, but not always, stated in the first sentence. Supporting ideas help to explain the main idea. They answer questions about the main idea, such as how, why, what, and when. As you read, it is helpful to identify the main ideas of paragraphs in a passage, and distinguish them from supporting ideas.

Which of these sentences best expresses the main idea of paragraph C of Reading 1?

a. Both primates and humans tend to spend more time being cooperative than they do fighting with one another.

b. Chimpanzees typically spend their days traveling together and taking care of one another.

Sentence **a** best expresses the main idea of the paragraph. Sentence **b** expresses a supporting idea: It helps to explain the main idea by providing an example.

IDENTIFYING
MAIN AND
SUPPORTING IDEAS

A Read the following paragraph about gorilla behavior. Is each sentence (1–4) a main idea or a supporting idea? Write **M** for Main Idea or **S** for Supporting Idea. One is extra.

Scientists have found that male gorillas in the forests of northern Congo splash water to help them find a mate. Richard Parnell, a primate researcher at the University of Stirling, observed that male gorillas intimidate other males and try to get the attention of females by splashing water with their hands. In one type of splashing behavior, for example, male gorillas raise one or both arms and hit the surface of the water with their palms open. Using water in this way, Parnell says, shows that gorillas are "adaptable, innovative, and intelligent creatures."

_____ 1. Male gorillas sometimes hit the water with their palms open.

_____ 2. Parnell says that splashing proves that gorillas are capable creatures.

_____ 3. Splashing water helps scare off other males.

_____ 4. Larger male gorillas are usually more successful at finding mates.

_____ 5. A study shows that male gorillas splash water to attract female gorillas.

IDENTIFYING
MAIN AND
SUPPORTING IDEAS

B Look at your answers to exercise A. How do you know which sentences are supporting ideas? What questions (why, how, where, what) do they answer about the main idea? Discuss with a partner.

APPLYING

C Look back at paragraph G of Reading 1. Underline a main idea of the paragraph and two ideas that support it.

Video

ELEPHANT ORPHANS

A shelter in Kenya cares for young elephants that have lost their parents.

BEFORE VIEWING

A Read the photo caption. What kind of care do you think the elephant orphans need? Discuss with a partner.

PREDICTING

B Read the information about the illegal ivory trade and answer the questions. Then discuss them with a partner.

LEARNING ABOUT THE TOPIC

One of the biggest dangers facing African elephants is hunting by poachers—people who illegally catch or kill animals for profit. Poachers kill elephants so they can remove and sell their valuable ivory tusks. Ivory is usually made into jewelry and art objects. Although the ivory trade is banned in most countries, ivory is often smuggled[1] in and sold illegally. Between 2010 and 2012, poachers killed over 100,000 African elephants. In Central Africa, the elephant population has decreased by 64 percent in a decade. Poachers have shortened these animals' life spans and disrupted their close communities.

[1]**smuggled:** brought into or out of another country or area illegally

1. Why do you think people continue to buy objects made of ivory?

   _____

2. What do you think could be done to stop the illegal ivory trade?

   _____

   _____

C The words in **bold** are used in the video. Read the paragraph. Then match the correct form of each word to its definition.

The David Sheldrick Wildlife Trust in Nairobi, Kenya, takes care of orphan elephants. Many of these elephants are orphans because poachers **slaughtered** their mothers. **Caretakers** at the Trust stay with the orphans 24 hours a day, in order to provide them with plenty of **maternal** interaction. The organization's goal is the **reintroduction** of the elephants back into the wild.

1. _____ (adj) like a mother

2. _____ (v) to kill in large numbers

3. _____ (n) a person responsible for looking after someone or something

4. _____ (n) the act of putting something back into an environment where it once was

WHILE VIEWING

A ▶ Watch the video. What is one of the biggest challenges that the David Sheldrick Wildlife Trust faced in keeping the baby elephants alive? Circle the best answer.

a. getting them to trust humans

b. keeping them warm

c. learning what to feed them

B ▶ Watch the video again. Write answers to the following questions.

1. According to the video, what are two things baby elephants need?

_____

2. What is one way caretakers try to copy an elephant's relationship with its mother?

_____

3. What are three ways human and elephant babies are similar?

_____

_____

AFTER VIEWING

A Discuss these questions with a partner.

1. At the end of the video, the narrator says, "These orphans are all safe here—for the time being." Why do you think the narrator uses the phrase "for the time being"?

2. How effective do you think elephant orphanages are in addressing the issue of poaching? Why?

B Write one behavior that both primates and elephants have in common with humans. Use information from the video and Explore the Theme.

_____

Reading 2

PREPARING TO READ

A The words and phrases in **blue** below are used in Reading 2. Read the sentences. Then match the correct form of each word or phrase to its definition.

> Researchers have **observed** that children **generally** sleep better when parents **establish** a regular bedtime routine.
>
> **Previously**, it was common for **extended families** to live together in one home. But today, fewer people live with their grandparents or other relatives.
>
> Coyotes and wolves have similar **social structures**—both live in family groups.
>
> It's normal for children, regardless of **gender**, to have an **intense** feeling of fear when they are separated from their parents. These strong feelings often go away with time.
>
> One way to **discipline** children is to send them to their rooms alone.
>
> When animals shed their fur, new fur grows to **replace** the fur that is lost.

1. _____ (adv) usually

2. _____ (adj) very great or extreme

3. _____ (n) a group that includes uncles, cousins, grandparents, etc.

4. _____ (n) the way a group of people or animals is organized

5. _____ (n) the characteristics of being male or female

6. _____ (v) to create or start something that will last a long time

7. _____ (v) to train someone to follow rules or codes of behavior

8. _____ (v) to notice something after looking closely

9. _____ (v) to have something new or different instead of the original

10. _____ (adv) before the time period that you are talking about

B Discuss these questions with a partner.

1. What are two ways in which **establishing** a routine can make your life easier?

2. What are some benefits of living in an **extended family**? What are some drawbacks?

C Read the title and the subheadings in the reading passage. What links the three stories together? Check your idea as you read.

a. male and female roles in animal societies

b. scientific research of primates in Africa

c. animal societies in which females have power

GENDER IN THE WILD

🎧 Track 2

A   How does gender impact family relationships in the wild? Recent studies show how gender influences the social structure of elephants, geladas, and chimps.

Studies Show Gender Effect in Elephant Societies

Young elephants grow up in extended matriarchal[1] families. Elephant mothers, aunts, grandmothers, and female friends cooperate to raise babies in large, carefully organized **B** groups. This system helps protect young orphan elephants when hunters or farmers kill their mothers. When a young elephant is orphaned, other females take over the dead mother's role. The strong bonds between

females continue throughout their lives, which can be as long as 70 years. In contrast, young male elephants stay close to their female family members until they are 14. Then they generally leave their mothers and form other groups with male elephants.

Previously, male elephants were perceived to be less social than females. However, a recent **C** study at Etosha National Park in Namibia shows that males often form intense, long-lasting friendships with other males. During

[1] In a **matriarchal** family or group, the rulers are female and power is passed from mother to daughter.

A female African elephant bonds with her baby.

Gelada Study Reveals Female Primates with Power

Geladas are primates that live in the remote highlands of Ethiopia. Males are larger than females, but females have the real power in family groups. Wildlife biologist Chadden Hunter studies geladas in Simen Mountains National Park in Ethiopia. Hunter has observed that typical family units have between
D two and eight adult females, their offspring, and a primary male, which researchers call the family male. Gelada males have little say in what the family does from day to day. The females decide where and how long to graze[3] for food, when to move, and where to sleep. They also choose which male will be their mate and when it is time to replace that mate.

Young bachelor[4] males live in separate groups. They spend most of their time observing family groups and looking for
E opportunities to challenge the family males. When a young bachelor comes too close to a family, the family male chases him away.

[3] When animals **graze**, they eat the grass or other plants that are growing in a particular place.
[4] A **bachelor** is a single male without a female partner or children.

the study, Stanford University behavioral psychologist Caitlin O'Connell-Rodwell found that each member knew his status, and that the group followed a strict social hierarchy. Older males act as teachers and mediators[2] for younger ones, controlling or disciplining them when conflict occurs. These strict rules of behavior are helpful when food and drink are scarce. O'Connell-Rodwell observed that "in dry years, the strict pecking order they establish benefits all of them." For example, the young bulls know they must get in line behind the more senior elephants. In this way, everyone gets a turn to eat and drink, conflict is avoided, and peace is maintained.

[2] A **mediator** is someone who helps two people or groups solve an issue or a problem.

In gelada societies, females are the real decision-makers.

Young female chimps may care for sticks like mother chimps care for their babies.

To replace a family male, the females invite a bachelor into the family. Females typically do this when a family male becomes weak or does not give enough attention to them or their offspring. Hunter explains, "That's especially true in families where there are six or seven females; it's a lot of work to keep them all happy."

Hunter has observed that no family male lasts more than four years, and many are replaced before three. However, replaced males do not leave their families. Rather, they stay on in a kind of grandfather role. "That way, they can protect their children," he says, "and they're very aggressive about that." Hunter's study has generated new interest in geladas, and it will challenge primatologists to learn more about their gender behavior.

Researchers Discover Gender-Driven Play in Chimps

Just as human children often choose different toys, some monkeys in captivity have demonstrated gender-driven toy preferences. For example, young female vervet and rhesus monkeys often play with dolls in captivity, while young males prefer toys such as trucks. Now, for the first time, a study in Kibale National Park in Uganda shows that the same is true for chimps in the wild.

Richard Wrangham, a primatologist at Harvard University, has been studying the play behavior of male and female chimps. His team observed that the way a community of young Kanyawara female chimps played with sticks mimicked caretaking behaviors. The young females took sticks to their nests and cared for them like mother chimps with their babies. The chimps appeared to be using the sticks as dolls, as if they were practicing for motherhood. This play preference, which was very rarely seen in males, was observed in young female chimps more than a hundred times during 14 years of study. In contrast, young males did not normally play with objects. Instead, they preferred active play—climbing, jumping, and chasing each other through trees.

Stick play may have evolved to prepare females for motherhood. It may have given them an advantage by providing skills and knowledge that contributed to their survival. It is also possible that stick play is just an expression of the imagination—an ability found in chimps and humans but few other animals.

UNDERSTANDING THE READING

A Choose the sentence that best expresses the main idea of each section in the passage.

UNDERSTANDING MAIN IDEAS

1. **Studies Show Gender Effect in Elephant Societies**

    a. Both male and female elephants have an excellent memory and are able to remember elephants they meet.

    b. Female elephants are in charge of raising families, while males form hierarchical groups with other males.

2. **Gelada Study Reveals Female Primates with Power**

    a. Female geladas control family groups in gelada society.

    b. There is a strict hierarchy within female geladas in a single family.

3. **Researchers Discover Gender-Driven Play in Chimps**

    a. The types of play that young chimps prefer seem to be related to gender.

    b. Young chimps learn their social skills by playing with their mothers.

B Complete the main ideas (M) and supporting ideas (S) from "Gelada Study Reveals Female Primates with Power." Write no more than three words in each space.

IDENTIFYING MAIN AND SUPPORTING IDEAS

Paragraph D

   M: Female geladas have _____ in family groups.

     S1: Family groups have a large number of geladas.

     S2: Female geladas decide what the family does _____ .

     S3: Female geladas choose their _____ .

Paragraph E

   M: Nonfamily male geladas live in _____ .

     S1: Bachelor males wait for a chance to challenge the _____ .

     S2: Female geladas _____ bachelor males when they want to.

Paragraph F

   M: Most family males are _____ after a few years.

     S: The old family males _____ in the family group.

C Complete each sentence with details from the reading passage. Write no more than three words in each space.

UNDERSTANDING DETAILS

Studies Show Gender Effect in Elephant Societies

1. In male elephant groups, each member knows his _____ .

2. _____ discipline young male elephants when they fight.

Gelada Study Reveals Female Primates with Power

3. In a typical gelada family, there is one _____ .

4. When the family male is replaced, he usually takes on a _____ role.

Researchers Discover Gender-Driven Play in Chimps

5. Young females play with sticks, while young males tend to prefer _____ .

6. Playing with sticks may prepare young female chimps for _____ .

D What evidence does the author use in "Researchers Discover Gender-Driven Play in Chimps"? Complete the statements below. Then discuss your ideas with a partner.

1. The article describes a _____ in Kibale National Park as evidence for gender-driven play in chimps.

2. The expert who did the chimp study is Richard Wrangham, a _____ from Harvard University.

3. Wrangham's team observed that female chimps' stick play was similar to _____ behaviors.

4. Wrangham's study lasted _____ years. During this time, his team observed the same behavior more than _____ times.

E Discuss these questions with a partner.

1. Do you think the supporting evidence in exercise D is convincing? Why or why not?

2. Compare the three reports in the passage. Which one do you think provides the most convincing supporting evidence? Why?

F Find and underline these words and phrases in the passage. Use context to identify their meanings. Then complete the sentences with a suitable form of the words and phrases.

pecking order (paragraph C)	in captivity (paragraph G)
offspring (paragraph D)	mimicked (paragraph H)

1. Hyenas live in groups with a strict _____. One female has the most power and makes all of the decisions for the group.

2. Researchers saw that a baby chimp _____ her mother's behavior.

3. A mother emperor penguin protects her _____ from the Antarctic cold by keeping it under a warm layer of feathered skin.

4. It is difficult to study animals in the wild, but it is easy to study animals _____.

G Compare the animal species you learned about in this unit. Check (✓) the column(s) that apply to each species. Discuss the reasons for your answers with a partner.

Species	Females Control the Group	Hierarchy Is Important	Forming Strong Bonds Is Important
chimpanzees			
elephants			
geladas			

Writing

EXPLORING WRITTEN ENGLISH

A Read the sentences below. Write **S** for sentences that show similarities. Write **D** for sentences that show differences.

NOTICING

1. _____ As both humans and other primates tend to live in social groups, they may share some characteristics in terms of their social behavior.

2. _____ Young people may speak softly or avoid eye contact when they are talking to people with higher status. Similarly, when chimpanzees approach a powerful or senior member, they try to make themselves look smaller.

3. _____ A male gorilla usually has the power in a gorilla family group. In contrast, females make the decisions in a gelada family group.

4. _____ Human boys and girls often choose different toys. Likewise, young chimps in captivity have shown gender-driven toy preferences.

5. _____ Unlike young female chimps, young males did not normally play with objects.

LANGUAGE FOR WRITING Making Comparisons

Use these expressions to show similarities.

> Office workers **are similar** to primates. **Both** use conflict and cooperation in groups.
>
> Humans generally live in harmony. **Likewise / Similarly**, chimpanzees try to avoid conflict.
>
> **Like** humans, chimpanzees may limit aggression to avoid isolation.

Use these expressions to show differences.

> **While** aggression is part of normal primate behavior, it plays a limited role in the wild.
>
> The strong bonds among female elephants continue throughout their lives. **In contrast**, young male elephants stay close to their female family members only until they are 14.
>
> Elephant families are matriarchal. **On the other hand**, males traditionally have the power in gorilla groups.
>
> Young male elephants live with their female family members, **whereas** older males form their own groups.
>
> **Unlike** young male chimps, who prefer active play, young female chimps have a preference for playing with sticks.

Note:

• The form of *be* in *be similar to* must agree with its subject.
• Use *likewise* and *similarly* at the beginning of sentences, followed by a comma.
• *In contrast* and *on the other hand* can appear at the beginning of sentences, followed by a comma. They can also appear after the subject. Note the use of commas in this case: *Males, on the other hand, traditionally have the power in many human cultures.*

B Underline the words and phrases in exercise A that show similarities and differences.

C Complete the sentences with suitable words or phrases for making comparisons. Add commas if necessary.

1. Female geladas hold the power in the family. _____ males have little say about what goes on in the family.

2. Social networking is important in the human workplace. _____ chimpanzees form strong bonds within their groups.

3. Male geladas are big and have bushy manes _____ female geladas are small and less distinctive-looking.

4. Young male chimps prefer active play. Young female chimps _____ prefer less active play.

5. Humans have invented tools to help them survive. _____ chimpanzees make and use tools for specific purposes.

D Use the expressions in the Language for Writing box to write three sentences comparing elephants, chimpanzees, and geladas. Use the information from the chart in exercise G in Understanding the Reading 2.

_____

_____

_____

_____

WRITING SKILL Writing Body Paragraphs

An essay is a piece of writing that presents information and ideas on a topic. It typically has the following structure:

Introductory paragraph ⟶ Body paragraphs ⟶ Concluding paragraph

You will learn more about the introductory and concluding paragraphs in Unit 4. An essay has two or more **body paragraphs**. Each one expresses one main idea. A good body paragraph includes a topic sentence that presents the paragraph's main idea. It also includes supporting ideas that develop the main idea. Explanations, details, and examples give further information about the supporting ideas.

In a comparison essay, one way to organize body paragraphs is the point-by-point method. With this method, you discuss one **point of comparison** in each paragraph. For example, in an essay comparing wolves and dogs:

Body paragraph 1   the animals' relationships with humans

Body paragraph 2   the social structures of both animals

Below are typical ways to organize body paragraphs for a comparison essay:

Body paragraph 1		**Body paragaph 2**
a similarity	⟶	another similarity
a difference	⟶	another difference
a similarity	⟶	a difference

E Read the body paragraph below. Answer the questions and then discuss your answers with a partner.

One way that dogs and wolves differ is in their relationships with humans. Dogs are generally friendly and helpful around humans. This is probably because they have been living closely with humans for thousands of years. No one knows exactly why early wolves (ancestors of dogs) approached humans and began living with them, but these tamer individuals gradually evolved into the dogs we know today. Over time, dogs and humans developed a mutually beneficial relationship: humans sheltered and fed dogs, and dogs did jobs for humans. For example, dogs helped early humans hunt. Wolves, on the other hand, are shy and fearful of humans. One reason for this is that wolves are generally afraid of anything that is unfamiliar. This tendency most likely evolved as a survival strategy. Anything unfamiliar in a wolf's environment is a potential danger, so this fear helps it avoid threats to its existence. As a result, wolves are less likely to interact with humans.

1. Does the body paragraph focus mainly on a similarity or a difference?

   _____

2. Read the following thesis statement. Which of the two points of comparison does the body paragraph explain? Underline it.

   *While wolves and dogs are similar in some ways, the two animals are different in terms of **their relationships with humans** and **their social structures**.*

3. In the paragraph above, underline and label:
   a. the topic sentence
   b. a supporting idea about dogs
   c. a supporting idea about wolves
   d. an example that shows dogs' relationship with humans
   e. an explanation for wolves' behavior

The ancestors of the Mexican wolf were likely the first wolves to arrive in North America.

REVISING PRACTICE

The drafts below are the second body paragraph for the thesis statement in exercise E on page 21.

What did the writer do in Draft 2 to improve the paragraph? Match the changes (a–d) to the highlighted parts.

a. added a supporting detail
b. corrected language for making comparisons

c. added a topic sentence
d. deleted unrelated information

Draft 1

Wolves in the wild live in social groups called "packs." A wolf pack is made up of a male and female "alpha" pair—the leaders of the pack—and the alpha pair's offspring and extended family. Most wolves live in the United States, Canada, and Russia. Wolves live this way mainly because they have to hunt for their food, and packs hunt more successfully than individuals. Their clear hierarchy helps them cooperate in hunts and avoid fighting over food within the group. Unlike wolves need to live in packs, dogs do not. This is because, unlike wolves, dogs do not need to hunt to survive. Dogs in the wild search for food scraps left by humans or other animals on their own. Domestic dogs are fed by their human owners. Even when two or more dogs live together in a house, there is no alpha in the group. The dogs deal with conflict on a case-by-case basis, and any member of the group can breed.

Draft 2

Another way that wolves and dogs differ is in their social structures. Wolves in the wild live in social groups called "packs." A wolf pack is made up of a male and female "alpha" pair—the leaders of the pack—and the alpha pair's offspring and extended family. Wolves live this way mainly because they have to hunt for their food, and packs hunt more successfully than individuals. Their clear hierarchy helps them cooperate in hunts and avoid fighting over food within the group. The alphas eat first, make all the decisions for the pack, and are the only ones in the pack that breed. While wolves need to live in packs, dogs do not. This is because, unlike wolves, dogs do not need to hunt to survive. Dogs in the wild search for food scraps left by humans or other animals on their own. Domestic dogs are fed by their human owners. Even when two or more dogs live together in a house, there is no alpha in the group. The dogs deal with conflict on a case-by-case basis, and any member of the group can breed.

EDITING PRACTICE

Read the information below.

In sentences with comparison expressions, remember:

- that the form of *be* in *be similar to* must agree with its subject.
- to use commas correctly in sentences with *while*, *like*, *likewise*, *similarly*, *on the other hand*, *unlike*, *whereas*, and *in contrast*.

Correct one mistake with comparison expressions in each of the sentences (1–5).

1. The use of tools among gorillas are similar to the use of tools among chimpanzees.

2. Dogs are not capable of using language. In contrast some apes are able to communicate using human sign language.

3. Horses help farmers by pulling carts. Likewise dogs help by herding sheep.

4. Cats in the wild have to hunt for food. House cats on the other hand, get their food from humans.

5. Chimpanzee mothers and daughters form strong bonds. Similarly adult female elephants form close relationships with young females in the family.

UNIT REVIEW

Answer the following questions.

1. What is one similarity between human office workers and chimpanzees?

   _____

   _____

   _____

2. What should you include in a body paragraph?

   _____

   _____

   _____

3. Do you remember the meanings of these words? Check (✔) the ones you know. Look back at the unit and review the ones you don't know.

   Reading 1:

   ☐ aggressive   ☐ ambitious   ☐ behavior

   ☐ care for   ☐ conflict   ☐ criticize

   ☐ interact   ☐ motivation AWL ☐ status

   ☐ treat

   Reading 2:

   ☐ discipline   ☐ establish   ☐ extended family

   ☐ gender AWL   ☐ generally   ☐ intense AWL

   ☐ observe   ☐ previously   ☐ replace

   ☐ social structure

Comparison Essays

In Nunavut, Canada, a sledder holds a photograph of a South Carolina swamp to show how different the Arctic looked 56 million years ago.

OBJECTIVES To learn how to write a comparison essay
To use connectors to show comparison and contrast
To use adverb clauses

Can you compare or contrast two places on earth?

What Is a Comparison Essay?

In a **comparison essay**, you can compare ideas, people, different times in history, or other things. The subjects of this kind of essay are two items that are related in some way. You can focus on the similarities between the two items, on the differences, or on both the similarities and the differences. Your goal is to show your readers how these items are similar or different, what their strengths and weaknesses are, or what their advantages and disadvantages are. In a history class, your essay might compare the French Revolution and the American Revolution. In an economics class, you might write about the similarities and differences between capitalism and socialism. In an art class, you might write about the differences in the works of two impressionist painters, such as Monet and Renoir.

Like other essays, the comparison essay has an introductory paragraph that contains a hook and a thesis statement, two or three or more paragraphs that make up the body, and a concluding paragraph.

Girl with a Fan by Pierre-Auguste Renoir

Banks of the Seine, Vétheuil, by Claude Oscar Monet

Patterns of Organization

There are two basic ways to organize a comparison essay—the block method and the point-by-point method.

Block Method	Point-by-Point Method
With the **block method**, you present one subject and all its points of comparison; then you do the same for the second subject. With this organization, you discuss each subject completely without interruption.	With the **point-by-point method**, you include both subjects in one point of comparison before moving on to the next point of comparison.
Introduction: Hook + thesis (Paragraph 1) **Body:** Supporting Information **Paragraph 2:** Renoir's inspirations, painting style, and most famous works. **Paragraph 3:** Monet's inspirations, painting style, and most famous works.	**Introduction:** Hook + thesis (Paragraph 1) **Body:** Supporting Information **Paragraph 2:** artistic inspirations (of Renoir and Monet) **Paragraph 3:** painting styles (of Renoir and Monet) **Paragraph 4:** Most famous works (of Renoir and Monet)
Conclusion: Conclusion (restated information + suggestion or opinion) (Paragraph 4)	**Conclusion:** (restated information + suggestion or opinion) (Paragraph 5)

Parallel Organization of Supporting Information

In the block-method example, notice that the supporting information in Paragraph 2 includes inspirations, painting style, and most famous works. The supporting information in Paragraph 3 also includes these three aspects of the artist. In the point-by-point method, the supporting information includes inspirations, painting style, and most famous works as well, but information about both artists is presented in one setting before going on to discuss both artists in the next setting.

These repeated structures are called parallel organization. No matter which overall method of organization you choose, parallel organization is required of your information in all comparison essays.

Choosing a Method of Organization

Review the two methods of organizing a compare-contrast essay and answer the questions.

1. What are the advantages of the block method for the writer? For the reader?

2. What are the advantages of the point-by-point method for the writer? For the reader?

ACTIVITY 1 Studying a Comparison Essay

This essay compares some features of Brazil and the United States. Discuss the Preview Questions with a partner. Then read the essay and answer the questions that follow.

Preview Questions

1. What do you know about the different cultural groups who live in Brazil and the United States?

2. What does the word *individualism* mean to you?

Essay 1

Not as Different as One Would Think

1   All countries in the world are unique. Obviously, countries are different from one another in location, size, culture, government, climate, and lifestyle. However, many countries share some surprising similarities. Some may think that these two nations have nothing in common because Brazil and the United States are in different **hemispheres**. On the contrary, they share many similarities.

a hemisphere: one half of the world

2   One important similarity is their size. Both Brazil and the United States are large countries. Brazil covers almost half of the South American continent. Few Brazilians can say that they have traveled **extensively** within the country's borders. Because Brazil covers such a large geographic area, its weather varies greatly from one area to another. Like Brazil, the United States takes up a significant portion of its continent (North America), so most Americans have visited only a few of the 50 states. In addition, the United States has a wide range of **climates**. When the Northeast is experiencing snowstorms, cities like Miami, Florida, can have temperatures over 85 degrees Fahrenheit.

extensively: widely, over a large area

the climate: the usual weather of a region

3   Another similarity between Brazil and the United States is the **diversity** of ethnic groups. Brazil was colonized by Europeans, and its culture has been greatly influenced by this fact. However, the identity of the Brazilian people is not **solely** a product of Western civilization. Brazil is a "melting pot" of many ethnic groups that immigrated there and mixed with the **indigenous** people. The United States also has a diversity of ethnic groups representing the early colonists from northern Europe as well as groups from Africa, the Mediterranean, Asia, and South America. The mixture of cultures and **customs** has worked to form ethnically rich cultures in both countries.

diversity: variety

solely: exclusively

indigenous: native, original

a custom: a learned social or cultural behavior

4   Finally, **individualism** is an important value for both Brazilians and Americans. Brazil works hard to defend the **concept** of freedom of choice. Citizens believe that they have the right to do and be whatever they desire as long as they do not hurt others. Individualism and freedom of choice also exist in the United States, where freedom is perhaps the highest value of the people. Some people may believe that the desire for individual expression is divisive and can make a country weak. However, the ability of people to be whatever they want makes both countries strong.

individualism: uniqueness, independence

a concept: an idea

5   Although Brazil and the United States are unique countries, there are **remarkable** similarities in their size, ethnic diversity, and personal values. Some people tend to believe that their culture and country are without equal. Nevertheless, it is important to remember that people as a whole have more in common than they generally think they do.

remarkable: amazing, extraordinary

Post-Reading

1. What two subjects does the writer compare in this essay?

   _____

2. What method of organization does the writer use—point-by-point or block?

   _____

3. What is the hook for this essay? Write it here.

   _____

   _____

   _____

4. Underline the thesis statement. Is the thesis restated in the conclusion (Paragraph 5)? If yes, underline the sentence in the conclusion that restates the thesis.

5. In Paragraph 2, the author writes about the ways in which size affects Brazil and the United States. In the following chart, list the supporting information the writer uses.

The Effects of Size	
Brazil	United States
a. _____	a. _____
_____	_____
b. _____	b. _____
_____	_____
c. _____	c. _____
_____	_____

6. Reread the concluding paragraph of "Not as Different as One Might Think." Does the writer offer a suggestion, an opinion, or a prediction? _____ Write the concluding sentence here.

_____

_____

Developing a Comparison Essay

In this next section, you will develop a comparison essay as you make an outline, write supporting information, and study connectors.

ACTIVITY 2 Outlining Practice

Below is a specific outline for "Not as Different as One Might Think." Some of the information is missing. Reread the essay beginning on page 28 and complete the outline.

Title: _____

I. Introduction (Paragraph 1)

A. Hook: _All countries in the world *are* unique._____

B. Connecting information: Different location, size, culture, government, climate, lifestyle

C. Thesis statement: _____

_____

II. Body

A. Paragraph 2 (Similarity 1) topic sentence: _____

_____

    1. Brazil's characteristics

        a. Size: _____

        b. Travel: Few Brazilians have traveled extensively in their country.

        c. Climate: _____

    2. _____

        a. _____

        b. Travel: _____

        c. Climate: The weather can be extremely different in the northern and the southern parts of the country.

B. Paragraph 3 (Similarity 2) topic sentence: Another similarity is the diversity of ethnic groups.

    1. Brazil

        a. _____

        b. Other ethnic groups

        c. _____

    2. United States

        a. Europe

        b. Africa

        c. the Mediterranean

        d. _____

        e. _____

C. Paragraph 4 (Similarity 3) topic sentence: _____

_____

    1. Brazilians' belief in freedom: _____

_____

    2. _____

_____

III. Conclusion (Paragraph 5)

    A. Restated thesis: _____

    _____

    B. Opinion: Nevertheless, it is important to remember that people as a whole have more in common than they generally think they do.

ACTIVITY 3 **Supporting Information**

The following comparison essay is missing the supporting information. Work with a partner to write supporting sentences for each paragraph. If you need more space, use a separate piece of paper. After you finish, compare your supporting information with that of other students. (Note: This essay follows the point-by-point organizational pattern.)

Essay 2

On the Desk or on the Lap?

1   Some years ago, buying a computer was considered by many to be a very frightening task. For one, personal computing was advanced technology that was being advertised to the general public for the first time. These computers were also extremely expensive, and to tell the truth, many consumers did not know whether these devices would one day be considered just a fad. History, of course, has shown that computers are here to stay. Computer technology has exceeded most people's expectations. Still, even today, computer shoppers need to know what their options are. One of the biggest considerations for a computer purchase is "desktop or laptop?" To reach a decision, a buyer can compare these two computer types in terms of their overall cost, convenience, and style.

2   Desktop computers and laptops differ in their costs. _____

_____

_____

_____

_____

_____

_____

_____

3   Another thing to consider is the convenience factor. _____

_____

_____

_____

_____

_____

_____

_____

4   Finally, there is the subject of style. _____

_____

_____

_____

_____

_____

_____

_____

5   Choosing between a desktop model and a laptop is a personal decision for the consumer. This decision can be made more easily by looking at the cost, convenience, and style preferences. While it can seem like a daunting task now, it will certainly become more and more difficult as new "species" of computers come on the market.

Writer's Note

Asking Questions

How can you develop details and facts that will support your main ideas (topic sentences) in each paragraph? One of the best ways to write this supporting information is to ask yourself questions about the topic—*Where? Why? When? Who? What? How?*

Grammar for Writing

Sentence Structure of Connectors (for Comparison Essays)

Writers use **connectors** to help clarify their main ideas. Connectors help readers by providing logical connections between sentences, ideas, and paragraphs. Notice that when these words, and often the phrase that follows them, begin a sentence, they are followed by a comma.

Connectors That Show Comparison Between Sentences of Paragraphs

Between Sentences of Paragraphs	Examples
In addition, Subject + Verb.	Both Red Beauty and Midnight Dream roses are known for the size of their blooms, their color, and their fragrance. **In addition**, they are easy to grow.
Similarly, Subject + Verb.	The Midnight Dream rose won awards in local contests last year. **Similarly**, the Red Beauty rose was singled out for its beauty.
Likewise, Subject + Verb.	The blooms of Red Beauty roses last longer than those of most other roses. **Likewise**, the blooms of the Midnight Dream rose are long lasting.
Compared to ... , Subject + Verb.	Some roses last for a very short time. **Compared to** these roses, the blooms of Red Beauty and Midnight Dream roses last a long time.

Connectors That Show Contrast Between Sentences of Paragraphs

Between Sentences of Paragraphs	Examples
However, Subject + Verb. *or* **On the other hand**, Subject + Verb.	Many differences are clear to even novice gardeners. **However / On the other hand**, some of their differences are not very obvious.
In contrast, Subject + Verb.	Red Beauty has a strong, sweet fragrance. **In contrast,** Midnight Dream's fragrance is light and fruity.
Although Subject + Verb, Subject + Verb.	Both Midnight Dream roses and Red Beauty roses are red. **Although** both varieties produce red flowers, Midnight Dream roses are much darker than Red Beauty roses.
Even though Subject + Verb, Subject + Verb.	Red Beauty roses and Midnight Dream roses are long-stemmed roses. **Even though** both of these species are long stemmed, Red Beauty stems are thin and covered with thorns while Midnight Dream stems are thick and have almost no thorns.
Unlike Noun, Subject + Verb.	What do we know about the cost of these two kinds of roses? **Unlike** Red Beauty, Midnight Dream roses are relatively inexpensive.

For a more complete list of connectors, see the *Brief Writer's Handbook*, pages 119–120.

Read the following student essay and circle the appropriate connector in each set of parentheses. Refer to the charts on page 35 if necessary.

The writer in this essay uses the block method of writing to compare two parenting styles.

Essay 3

Parenting 101

1   The film previews are finished, and the movie theater is quiet as everyone waits for the feature film to appear. (1. However / On the other hand), the **stillness** is suddenly broken by a noise. The audience hears a sniffle. The sniffle soon turns to a cry, then a wail. There is an uncomfortable, or perhaps unhappy, toddler sitting in the movie theater. People start shuffling uncomfortably in their seats as they wait for what will happen next. Will the child be taken out of the theater, or will the parent pretend that everything is ok? **Scenarios** like these happen regularly. **Bystanders** wonder what the parent or caretaker will do. The action, of course, often depends on the type of parenting styles that adults use with their children. The two **extremes** are the **lenient (laissez-faire)** parent and the strict disciplinarian parent.

2   Lenient parents often focus on their child's having fun and enjoying "being a kid." If a child does something careless like break a glass, lenient parents will not become angry or scream. They know that the child is probably experimenting and meant no harm. (2. Likewise / Otherwise), they may even explain to the child that it was an accident and the child should not be upset or cry. (3. In contrast / In addition), lenient parents may not be too concerned about time-based activities and schedules. They will allow their children to stay up late and experience new things. The motto "You're only a kid once!" rings very true to these free spirits. This

a stillness: silence; tranquility

a scenario: situation

a bystander: people who witness something but are not involved

an extreme: boundaries, opposites

lenient: easy-going; relaxed

laissez-faire: (French) "let it be" or "leave it alone"

type of parent sees themselves as guides for their children, which cannot be said about the second parenting group: the disciplinarians.

3   Disciplinarian parents consider themselves role models for their children. (4. Unlike / Similarly) laissez-faire parents, their main priorities are safety and protection of their children. In essence, children are **monitored** very carefully and may not be allowed to play outside, interact with animals, or rough-house in general. A child who experiences a strict upbringing may be encouraged to focus on his studies instead of making friends. (5. In addition / However), interaction may be limited to only close family members. Children who are raised in highly-disciplined environments are **poised** to do very well in school.

4   In the end, no parents are truly 100 percent lenient or 100 percent strict when it comes to raising their child. Most fall somewhere in the middle depending on the child, the environment, and the particular situation. Society knows that both **child-rearing** styles have advantages and disadvantages, but the more interesting question is this: Which style will these children choose when the time comes for them to become parents?

to monitor: observe, supervise

to be poised to: prepared to

child rearing: raising children, bringing up children

Building Better Vocabulary

ACTIVITY 5 **Word Associations**

Circle the word or phrase that is most closely related to the word or phrase on the left. If necessary, use a dictionary to check the meaning of words you do not know.

	A	B
1. diversity	difference	distance
2. customs	shirts	traditions
3. a concept	an idea	a traditional song
4. remarkable	amazing	repetitive
5. a hemisphere	in geography class	in math class
6. to rough-house	aggressive play	gentle play
7. monitor	create	observe
8. disciplinarian	lenient	strict
9. likewise	also	but
10. a climate	salary	weather

Fill in each blank with the word on the left that most naturally completes the phrase on the right. If necessary, use a dictionary to check the meaning of words you do not know.

1. make / pay   to _____ attention to something

2. task / way   a frightening _____

3. say / tell   to _____ the truth

4. find / reach   to _____ a decision

5. between / from   the differences _____ the two cities

6. personal / private   make a _____ decision

7. said / shown   history has _____

8. likewise / significant   a _____ portion

9. common / contrary   to have nothing in _____

10. crowds / groups   ethnic _____

Grammar for Writing

Using Adverb Clauses

Good writers use different types of sentences in their work, and sentence variety is certainly an important element in academic writing.

An adverb clause is a clause that indicates condition, contrast, reason, purpose, result, or a time relationship. An adverb clause begins with a connector called a subordinating conjunction. Examples of subordinating conjunctions are *if, although, after, since,* and *because*.

In the following sentences from essays in this book, the subordination conjunctions are circled and the adverb clauses are underlined.

(**Although**) Brazil and the United States are unique countries, there are remarkable similarities in their size, ethnic diversity, and personal values.

(**While**) it can seem like a daunting task now, it will certainly become more and more difficult as new "species" of computers come on the market.

(**When**) the Northeast is experiencing snowstorms, cities like Miami, Florida, can have temperatures over 85 degrees Fahrenheit.

(**If**) a child does something careless like break a glass, lenient parents will not become angry or scream.

Function	Subordinating Conjunctions (begin dependent clauses)	Transitions (usually precede independent clauses)
Concession	although even though though	Admittedly, Despite this, Even so, Nevertheless,
Contrast	although even though while	Conversely, In contrast, Instead, However, On the other hand,
Result	so so that	As a consequence, As a result, Consequently, Therefore, Thus,
Time Relationships	after as as soon as before until when whenever while	First, Second, Next, In the meantime, Meanwhile, Then, Finally, Subsequently, Afterward,
Cause / Reason	because since	
Condition	even if if provided that unless when	
Purpose	in order that so that	
Comparison		In the same way, Likewise, Similarly,
Examples		For example, In particular, Specifically, To illustrate,
Information		Furthermore, In addition, Moreover,
Refutation		On the contrary,

ACTIVITY 7 Identifying Adverb Clauses and Subordinating Conjunctions

Underline the six adverb clauses in these sentences from essays in this book. Circle the subordinating conjunctions. If a sentence does not have an adverb clause, write X on the line.

_____ 1. Unlike Red Beauty, Midnight Dream roses are relatively inexpensive.

_____ 2. When the Northeast is experiencing snowstorms, cities like Miami, Florida, can have temperatures over 85 degrees Fahrenheit.

_____ 3. Some may think that these two nations have nothing in common because Brazil and the United States are in different hemispheres.

_____ 4. Few Brazilians can say that they have traveled extensively within the country's borders.

_____ 5. Even though both of these species are long-stemmed, Red Beauty stems are thin and covered with thorns.

_____ 6. In contrast, lenient parents may not be too concerned about time-based activities and schedules.

_____ 7. If a child does something careless like break a glass, lenient parents will not become angry or scream.

_____ 8. People start shuffling uncomfortably in their seats as they wait for what will happen next.

_____ 9. Because Brazil covers such a large geographic area, its weather varies greatly from one area to another.

_____ 10. Nevertheless, it is important to remember that people as a whole have more in common than they generally think they do.

Developing Ideas for Writing

Brainstorming

You will be asked to write comparison essays in many of your classes. Often, you will be given the two subjects to be compared, such as two poems from a literature course, two political beliefs from a political science course, or an invention and a discovery from a history or science course. When you have to choose your own subjects for comparison, the following brainstorming tips will help you.

Tips for Brainstorming Subjects

1. **The subjects should have something in common.** For example, soccer and hockey are both fast-paced games that require a player to score a point by putting an object into a goal guarded by a player from the other team.
2. **The two subjects must also have some differences.** For example, the most obvious differences between the two games are the playing field, the protective equipment, and the number of players.
3. **You need to have enough information on each topic to make your comparisons.** If you choose two sports that are not well-known, it might be more difficult to find information about them.

Make a List

A good way to determine whether you have enough information about similarities and differences between two subjects is to brainstorm a list. Read the information in the lists below.

Ice Hockey	**Soccer**
played on ice	played on a grass field
six players on a team	11 players on a team
uses a puck	uses a soccer ball
(very popular sport)	(very popular sport)
(players use lots of protective pads)	(players use some protective pads)
(cannot touch the puck with your hands)	(cannot touch the ball with your hands)
(goal = puck in the net)	(goal = ball in the net)

As you can see, soccer and hockey have many similarities and a few differences. Notice that the similarities are circled. These are "links" between the two subjects. A writer could use these links to highlight the similarities between the two games or to lead into a discussion of the differences between them: "Although both soccer and hockey are popular, more schools have organized soccer teams than hockey. . . ."

Make a Venn Diagram

Another way to brainstorm similarities and differences is to use a Venn diagram. A Venn diagram is a visual representation of the similarities and differences between two concepts. Here is a Venn diagram of the characteristics of hockey and soccer.

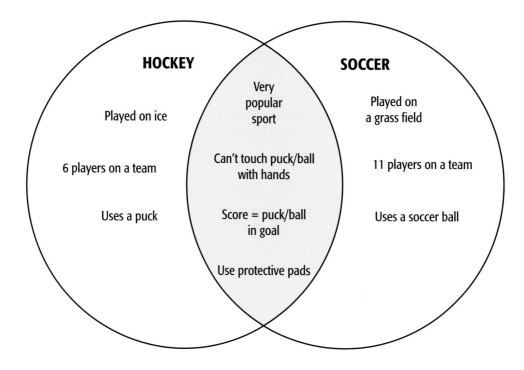

HOCKEY

Played on ice

6 players on a team

Uses a puck

Very popular sport

Can't touch puck/ball with hands

Score = puck/ball in goal

Use protective pads

SOCCER

Played on a grass field

11 players on a team

Uses a soccer ball

ACTIVITY 8 **Identifying Good Topics for a Comparison Essay**

Below are pairs of potential subjects for a comparison essay. Write *yes* on the line under the pairs that would be good topics and explain briefly what characteristics could be compared. Write *no* under the topics that would not be good choices and change one or both of them into more suitable topics. The first two have been done for you.

1. living in a house / living in an apartment

   yes—compare costs, privacy, space _____

2. international travel / domestic travel

   _____

3. high school / college

   _____

4. the weather in Toronto / tourist attractions in Toronto

   _____

5. wild animals / animals in a zoo

   _____

6. computers / computer keyboards

   _____

7. hands / feet

_____

8. the surface of the ocean floor / the surface of the continents

_____

9. the Earth / the North American continent

_____

10. Chinese food / Mexican food

_____

Original Student Writing: Comparison Essay

ACTIVITY 9 **Working with a Topic**

Complete the following steps to develop ideas for a comparison essay.

1. Choose one topic from the list below or use your own idea for a topic. If you want to use an original idea, talk to your teacher to see if it is appropriate for a comparison essay.

two sports	two movies	two systems of education
two places	two machines	two kinds of professions
two desserts	two famous people	two celebrations or holidays

2. Use the following chart to brainstorm a list of information about each subject. If you like, use the list about soccer and hockey on page 41 as a guide.

TOPIC: _____	
Subject 1: _____	**Subject 2:** _____
_____	_____
_____	_____
_____	_____
_____	_____
_____	_____
_____	_____
_____	_____
_____	_____
_____	_____
_____	_____

3. Now fill in the Venn diagram using the information from the chart in Item 2 on page 43.

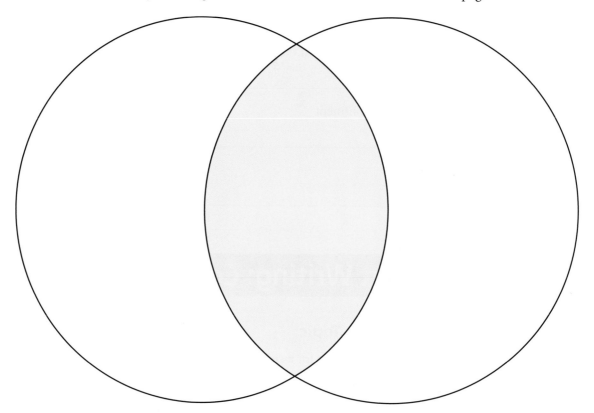

4. Decide if you are going to focus on the similarities or the differences between the two subjects or both in your comparison essay. Then choose three or four main points of comparison that you will use and list them here.

a. _____

b. _____

c. _____

d. _____

Writer's Note

Ideas for Supporting Information

In the next activity, you will develop supporting information. Here are some ideas to use as supporting information in your body paragraphs:

- give descriptions
- give examples
- explain the causes
- explain the effects

ACTIVITY 10 Planning with an Outline

Use the following outline to help you brainstorm a more detailed plan for your comparison essay. For this activity, use the point-by-point method of organization. Remember that the point-by-point method organizes each paragraph by one point of comparison, such as the languages, the populations, or the climates of two countries. Include your ideas from Activity 9. Write complete sentences where possible.

Topic: _____

I. Introduction (Paragraph 1)

   A. Hook: _____

       _____

   B. Connecting information: _____

       _____

       _____

   C. Thesis statement: _____

       _____

       _____

II. Body

   A. Paragraph 2 (first point of comparison) topic sentence: _____

       _____

SUPPORT

       1. _____

          a. _____

          b. _____

       2. _____

          a. _____

          b. _____

   B. Paragraph 3 (second point of comparison) topic sentence: _____

       _____

SUPPORT

       1. _____

          a. _____

          b. _____

       2. _____

          a. _____

          b. _____

C. Paragraph 4 (third point of comparison) topic sentence: _____

_____

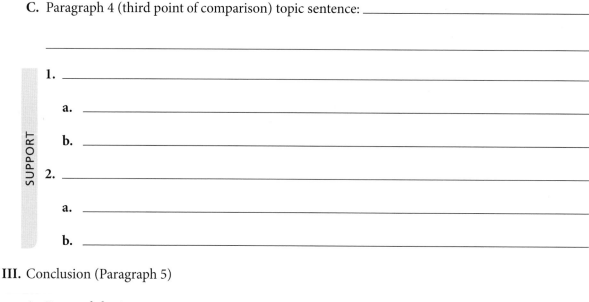

SUPPORT

1. _____
    a. _____
    b. _____
2. _____
    a. _____
    b. _____

III. Conclusion (Paragraph 5)

   A. Restated thesis: _____

   B. Suggestion, opinion, or prediction: _____

> If you need ideas for words and phrases, see the Useful Vocabulary for Better Writing on pages 121–124.

ACTIVITY 11 **Peer Editing Your Outline**

Exchange books with a partner and look at Activity 10. Read your partner's outline. Then use Peer Editing Sheet 1 on ELTNGL.com/sites/els to help you comment on your partner's outline. Use your partner's feedback to revise your outline. Make sure you have enough information to develop your supporting sentences.

ACTIVITY 12 **Writing a Comparison Essay**

Write a comparison essay based on your revised outline from Activity 10. Use at least two of the vocabulary words or phrases presented in Activities 5 and 6. Underline these words and phrases in your essay. Be sure to refer to the seven steps in the writing process in the *Brief Writer's Handbook* on pages 95–102.

ACTIVITY 13 **Peer Editing Your Essay**

Exchange papers from Activity 12 with a partner. Read your partner's essay. Then use Peer Editing Sheet 2 on ELTNGL.com/sites/els to help you comment on your partner's writing. Be sure to offer positive suggestions and comments that will help your partner improve his or her essay. Consider your partner's comments as you revise your own essay.

Additional Topics for Writing

Here are more ideas for topics for a comparison essay. Before you write, be sure to refer to the seven steps in the writing process in the *Brief Writer's Handbook*, pages 95–102.

PHOTO
TOPIC: Look at the photograph on pages 24–25. Compare or contrast two places on Earth. How are these places alike or different? Have you been to these places? If not, how did you learn about them?

TOPIC 2: Compare the situation in a country before and after an important historical event, such as Cuba before and after Fidel Castro came to power.

TOPIC 3: Discuss two kinds of music, such as classical and pop. A few points of comparison might be artists, instruments, audiences, and popularity.

TOPIC 4: Show how the world has changed since the invention of the cell (mobile) phone. How did people communicate before its invention? How easy or difficult was it to get in contact with someone?

TOPIC 5: Show the similarities and differences in the ways that two cultures celebrate an important event, such as a birthday, wedding, or funeral.

Timed Writing

How quickly can you write in English? There are many times when you must write quickly such as on a test. It is important to feel comfortable during those times. Timed-writing practice can make you feel better about writing quickly in English.

1. Take out a piece of paper.

2. Read the essay guidelines and the writing prompt.

3. Write a basic outline, including the thesis and your three main points.

4. Write a five-paragraph essay.

5. You have 40 minutes to write your essay.

Comparison Essay Guidelines

- Use the point-by-point method.

- Remember to give your essay a title.

- Double-space your essay.

- Write as legibly as possible (if you are not using a computer).

- Select an appropriate principle of organization for your topic.

- Include a short introduction (with a thesis statement), three body paragraphs, and a conclusion.

- Try to give yourself a few minutes before the end of the activity to review your work. Check for spelling, verb tense, and subject-verb agreement mistakes.

Compare two popular vacation destinations.

NOTES

RETHINKING BUSINESS 3

A "break out space" designed to encourage creativity among staff at Google's London office

ACADEMIC SKILLS

READING	Understanding sentences with initial phrases
GRAMMAR	Using sentences with initial phrases
CRITICAL THINKING	Understanding multiword units
WRITING SKILL	Organizing comparison essays

THINK AND DISCUSS

1 What are the most successful businesses in your country?

2 What made those businesses successful? How are those businesses different to other companies?

EXPLORE THE THEME

A Look at the information on these pages and answer the questions.

   1. Which country exports the most clothing? In which country do people spend the most on clothing?

   2. Which of the facts below is most interesting? Why?

B Match the correct form of the words in blue to their definitions.

   _____ (n) clothing

   _____ (n) the sale of goods to the public

   _____ (n) the financial gain a company or a person makes

   _____ (n) a person or business that you are competing with

FASHION FACTS

Fashion is big business. The global apparel market is valued at around 2.4 trillion dollars and accounts for 2 percent of the world's Gross Domestic Product (GDP).

These are the three largest fashion companies in the world—each making billions of dollars of profits each year. Nike's closest rival in the sportswear business, Adidas, is ranked number 5, after the fashion retail outlet, TJ Maxx.

1 Dior
$43.6 billion in sales

2 Nike
$33.8 billion in sales

3 Inditex
$25.7 billion in sales

There are **24.8 million** people in the world working to make clothes. China, the world's largest exporter of cloth and clothing, has over 10 million people working in the industry. They can make over 40 billion items of clothing in a year.

On average, Australians spend the most money on clothing.

Total Yearly Spending on Apparel Per Capita* (in US$) (2015):

1. Australia	$1,050
2. Canada	$831
3. Japan	$814
4. United States	$686
5. The European Union	$663
6. Brazil	$273
7. Russia	$272
8. China	$109

*Per capita means per person in the country.

The fashion industry has a huge impact on the environment. For example, it takes **2,700** liters of water to make just one cotton shirt. That's enough water for a person to drink for two and a half years!

A model showcases the hanbok, a form of traditional Korean dress. The traditional outfit has seen a growth in popularity in recent years. Hanbok purchases by women in South Korea increased by 80 percent between 2013 and 2016.

Reading

PREPARING TO READ

BUILDING
VOCABULARY

A The words in **blue** below are used in the reading passage. Match the correct form of each word to its definition.

Nearly 80 years ago, a woman named Yoon Dokjeong began selling hand-pressed camellia oil as a hair treatment in her home of Kaesong, in what is now North Korea.
As a boy, her son Suh Sunghwan worked alongside his mother as she taught him how to make skincare products from natural materials. In 1945, Suh Sunghwan **founded** the South Korean cosmetics company AmorePacific. The company has its **headquarters** in Seoul, South Korea, and owns 30 cosmetic **brands**, including Laneige and Annick Goutal. Today, Yoon Dokjeong's grandson, Suh Kyungbae, is the company's CEO (chief **executive** officer). A great success in a very **competitive** industry, AmorePacific earned a profit of 811.5 billion won (US$707.2 million) in 2016.

1. _____ (adj) describing a situation or activity in which people or companies are trying to be more successful than others

2. _____ (v) to start a company, institution, or other organization

3. _____ (n) a senior-level employee who is responsible for making important decisions for the company

4. _____ (n) a product (or group of products) with its own name

5. _____ (n) an organization or company's main offices or center of control

▶ **Suh Kyungbae speaks to the media during AmorePacific's 70th anniversary conference.**

B Complete each sentence with the correct form of a word or phrase in the box. Use a dictionary to help you.

competitor	marketing	merchandise
outsource	shortage	supply chain

1. _____ is the activity of promoting and advertising goods or services in order to encourage people to buy them.

2. A company's _____ is someone who is trying to sell similar goods or services to the same people.

3. When a company _____ something, it pays workers from outside the company to do the work or supply the things it needs or sells.

4. If there is a _____ of something, there is not enough of it.

5. The things or goods a person or company sells is their _____.

6. A(n) _____ is the process involved in moving a product from supplier to customer.

C Discuss these questions with a partner.

1. What famous clothing **brands** do you know? Make a list below.

   _____

   _____

2. What do you know about the companies that make your favorite clothing brands? When were they **founded**? Where are their **headquarters**?

D Look back at your list of clothing brands in **C**. What makes each brand special? Note your ideas below. Then discuss with a partner.

   _____

   _____

E Skim the reading passage. What is it mainly about? Circle the correct option. Then read the passage to check your answers.

a. It describes the challenges of starting a clothing company.

b. It compares one company with other similar companies.

c. It explains how clothing is designed and manufactured.

CHANGING FASHION

by Mike W. Peng

> In the world of fast fashion, rather than only releasing a few new collections each year, companies like Zara sell a never-ending cycle of trend-led clothing, all year round.

🎧 Track 3

A Zara is now one of the world's hottest fashion chains. **Founded** in 1975, its parent company,[1] Inditex, has become a leading global **apparel** retailer. Since its initial public offering (IPO)[2] in 2001, Inditex, which owns eight fashion **brands**, has doubled the number of its stores. It has quadrupled its sales to US$25.7 billion, and its **profits** have risen to over US$3 billion. Zara contributes two-thirds of Inditex's total sales. In this intensely **competitive** industry, the secret to Zara's success is that Zara excels in **supply chain** management. In fact, Zara succeeds by first breaking and then rewriting industry rules.

Industry rule number one: *The origins of a fashion house usually carry a certain cachet.*[3] This is why most European fashion houses have their **headquarters** in Paris or Milan. However,

B Zara does not hail from Italy or France—it is from Spain. Even within Spain, Zara is not based in a cosmopolitan city like Barcelona or Madrid. Its headquarters are in Arteixo, a town of only 25,000 people in a remote corner of northwestern Spain. Yet Zara is active not only throughout Europe, but also in Asia and North America. Currently, it has more than 5,000 stores in 88 countries, and these stores can be found in some truly pricey locations: the Champs-Elysees in Paris, Fifth Avenue in New York, Galleria in Dallas, Ginza in Tokyo, Queen's Road Central in Hong Kong, and Huaihai Road in Shanghai.

[1] A **parent company** is a company that owns smaller businesses.
[2] When a company has an **initial public offering**, it sells its stock to the public for the very first time.
[3] If something has a certain **cachet**, it has a quality that makes people admire it.

Rule number two: *Avoid stock-outs* (running out of in-demand items). From Zara's point of view, stock-outs are a good thing, since occasional **shortages** contribute to a shopper's urge to "buy now." At Zara, items sell out fast, with new products arriving at **retail** outlets twice a week. "If you see something and don't buy it," said one shopper, "you can forget about coming back for it because it will be gone." By giving just a short window of opportunity to purchase a limited quantity of **merchandise**, Zara's customers are motivated to visit the stores more frequently. In London, shoppers visit the average store four times a year, but frequent Zara 17 times. There is a good reason to do so, too: Zara makes and offers shoppers about 20,000 different items per year, about triple what stores like Gap do. "At Gap, everything is the same," said one Zara customer. "Buying from Zara, you'll never end up looking like someone else."

Rule number three: *Bombarding[4] shoppers with ads is a must.* Traditionally, stores like Gap and H&M spend an average of 4 percent of their total sales on ads. Zara takes a different approach. It devotes just 0.3 percent of its sales to ads. The high traffic[5] in its stores reduces the need for advertising in the media, so most of Zara's **marketing** serves as a reminder for shoppers to visit the stores.

Rule number four: *Outsource for cheaper production.* Stores like Gap and H&M do not own any production facilities. They pay other companies to make their products, sometimes in places far away from their headquarters. However, outsourcing production (mostly to Asia) requires a long lead time[6]—usually several months. In contrast, Zara once again deviated from the norm. By concentrating more than half of its production in-house—in Arteixo, Spain, and nearby, in Portugal and Morocco—Zara has

developed a super-responsive supply chain. This means it can design, produce, and deliver a new item of clothing to its stores in a mere 15 *days*, a pace that is unheard of in the industry. The best speed most of its **rivals** can achieve is two months. Also, outsourcing may not necessarily be "low cost." Errors in trend prediction can easily lead to unsold inventory,[7] forcing their retail stores to offer steep discounts. The industry average is to offer 40 percent discounts across all merchandise. In contrast, Zara's ability to design

[7]An **inventory** is a supply or stock of something—the number of items that a store has for sale.

[4]If you **bombard** someone with something, you make them face a great deal of it.
[5]When a place has **high traffic**, it is crowded and has many people coming and going.
[6]In the production process, the **lead time** is the period of time between the decision to make a product and the completion of actual production.

and make new clothes quickly means shorter lead times and an ever-changing inventory. So it sells more at full price, and—when it discounts—averages only 15 percent.

Rule number five: *Strive for efficiency through large batches*. By producing products in large quantities, as is the industry norm, companies can benefit from economies of scale.[8] Zara, however, intentionally deals in small batches. Because of

[8]**Economies of scale** refers to the proportionate savings in costs gained when the level of production increases.

the greater flexibility and speed this approach affords, Zara does not worry about missing the boat when it comes to trends. When new trends emerge, Zara can react quickly. Also, it runs its supply chain like clockwork with a fast but predictable rhythm: Every store places orders on Tuesday/Wednesday and Friday/Saturday. Trucks and cargo flights run on established schedules—like a bus service. From Spain, shipments reach most European stores in 24 hours, U.S. stores in 48 hours, and Asian stores in 72 hours. And it is not only store staff who know exactly when

Zara staff at the company's headquarters in Arteixo, Spain. Zara is able to design, make, and deliver new products to its stores in just over two weeks.

shipments will arrive, but regular customers too. This motivates them to check out the new merchandise more frequently, especially on the shipment arrival days, known by Zara fans as "Z days."

Certainly, Zara has no shortage of **competitors**. But few have successfully copied its fast fashion and flexible business model. "I would love to organize our business like Inditex [Zara's parent]," noted an **executive** from Gap, "but I would have to knock my company down and rebuild it from scratch." This does not mean Gap and other rivals are not trying to copy Zara. The question is how long it takes for Zara's rivals to out-Zara Zara.

Adapted from **Global Business** *4th Edition, by Mike W. Peng,* © *Cengage Learning 2015*

Mike W. Peng is the Jindal Chair of Global Business Strategy at the University of Texas at Dallas. A National Science Foundation (NSF) CAREER Award winner, Professor Peng is a fellow with the Academy of International Business and listed among Thomson Reuters' The World's Most Influential Scientific Minds.

ZARA: BIRTH OF A BRAND

In 1963, in the unremarkable seaside town of La Coruña, Spain, 27-year-old Amancio Ortega Gaona started a business making bathrobes. By 1975, Ortega had saved enough money from this business to open a clothing store in town. He named his store Zorba, after the movie *Zorba the Greek*. However, he soon learned that there was a bar in town called Zorba just a couple of blocks away. The bar owner thought that it might be confusing to have two businesses in town with the same name, so Ortega agreed to change the name of his store. The problem was that he had already made the letter molds for the store's sign. Rather than having new molds made, Ortega used some of the letters he already had molds for, and came up with a new name: Zara.

UNDERSTANDING THE READING

A Choose the statement that best summarizes the writer's main idea.

UNDERSTANDING
MAIN IDEAS

   a. Zara is successful because it follows established norms of the fashion industry.

   b. Zara has achieved success because it is run differently from other clothing companies.

   c. Zara owes its success to closely following the practices of other clothing companies.

B According to the passage, how does Zara operate its business? Check (✓) all that apply.

UNDERSTANDING
SUPPORTING IDEAS

  ☐ a. It manufactures small numbers of items at a time, so it can get them into stores quickly.

  ☐ b. It spends a lot of money on advertising.

  ☐ c. The company headquarters are based in a major city.

  ☐ d. Most Zara items are made in Spain or in nearby countries.

  ☐ e. It creates a certain cachet by charging high prices for clothing.

  ☐ f. It intentionally runs out of styles and replaces them with new ones.

> **CRITICAL THINKING** Some words are commonly grouped together to make **multiword units or phrases**. In these phrases, words often have different meanings than they do when they're used individually. It's important to learn these words as units and to use context to help you understand what they mean.

C Find and underline the following multiword phrases in the reading passage. Then circle the best meaning for each phrase.

CRITICAL THINKING:
UNDERSTANDING
MULTIWORD UNITS

  1. Something that **serves as a reminder** _____.

     a. distracts people from doing that thing

     b. helps people remember to do that thing

  2. Someone who has **deviated from the norm** has _____.

     a. followed well-established ways of doing things

     b. done something different from what was expected

  3. If you **miss the boat**, you _____.

     a. do not understand a new idea correctly

     b. are too late to take advantage of an opportunity

  4. If something operates **like clockwork**, it _____.

     a. works on a regular schedule

     b. has very complex working parts

  5. If you rebuild something **from scratch**, you build it _____.

     a. again, from the beginning

     b. in its old building, with some changes

D Complete the missing bars in the charts using information from the reading passage.

1. Inditex Sales:
2001 vs. Today

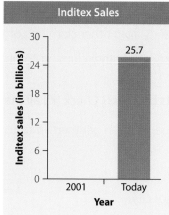

2. Average Store Visits per Year:
Zara vs. Average London Stores

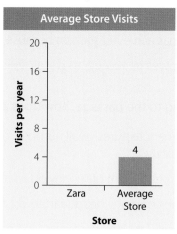

3. No. of Items Made per Year:
Zara vs. Gap

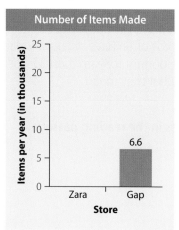

4. Spending on Advertising:
Zara vs. Gap / H&M

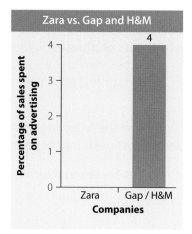

5. Days from Design to in Store:
Zara vs. Competitors

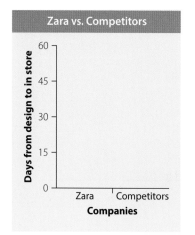

6. Discounts on Unsold Inventory:
Zara vs. Industry Average

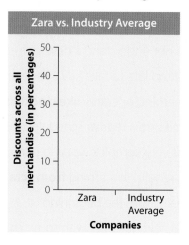

DEVELOPING READING SKILLS

> **READING SKILL** Understanding Sentences with Initial Phrases
>
> Writers often put prepositional, time, and verbal phrases at the beginnings of sentences, before the main clause. Writers use initial phrases to vary their sentence structure and to change the emphasis in a sentence.
>
> **Founded in 1975,** its parent company, Inditex, has become a leading global apparel retailer.
>
> **Since its initial public offering (IPO) in 2001,** Inditex, … has doubled the number of its stores.

A Look back at paragraphs C, D, E, and F in the reading passage. Find and underline all the initial phrases.

B Answer the questions. Use information from initial phrases you identified in **A**.

UNDERSTANDING SENTENCES WITH INITIAL PHRASES

1. Why are customers motivated to visit Zara stores more frequently than other stores?

   a. because items in Zara stores are only available for a relatively short time

   b. because Zara will regularly offer huge discounts on many of its products

2. How has Zara developed a super-responsive supply chain?

   a. by making most of its clothing in or near its headquarters

   b. by having factories in many different countries around the world

3. How do most fashion companies take advantage of economies of scale?

   a. by selling their items in huge stores

   b. by producing products in large batches

4. Why is Zara not worried about missing the boat when it comes to trends?

   a. because its designers are extremely good at predicting future fashion trends

   b. because it can keep up with trends by designing and making new products quickly

◄ **Boxes of ready-to-wear garments are prepared at Zara's headquarters in Arteixo, Spain.**

Italian fashion designer
Brunello Cucinelli

BEHIND THE BRAND

BEFORE VIEWING

DISCUSSION

A What famous fashion designers do you know? What are they known for? Discuss with a partner.

_____

_____

LEARNING ABOUT
THE TOPIC

B Read the information. Then answer the questions.

Brunello Cucinelli is a luxury Italian fashion brand that sells high-end menswear and womenswear in countries around the world. The company—best known for its cashmere sweaters—had humble beginnings. Founder Brunello Cucinelli first started out dying cashmere in a small workshop. After some success, he founded the company in 1978, and since then, the brand has gone from strength to strength. Nowadays, Cucinelli is a highly influential figure in the fashion industry, and in the last ten years, the company has quadrupled in size.

1. What kinds of fashion products does the company Brunello Cucinelli make?

   _____

2. What factors do you think make a fashion brand successful?

   _____

   _____

C The words in **bold** below are used in the video. Match the correct form of each word to its definition.

> Versace, Gucci, and Armani are three of the most famous **high-end** fashion brands.
>
> In many parts of the world, working conditions are improving thanks to **enlightened** business owners recognizing the importance of workers' rights.
>
> The rise of big businesses has led to fewer and fewer people being able to make a living as self-employed **artisans**.
>
> Calvin Klein founded his **eponymous** fashion brand in New York in 1968.

1. _____ (adj) named after a particular person

2. _____ (adj) expensive and luxurious

3. _____ (adj) having modern, well-informed opinions

4. _____ (n) someone who works with their hands in a skilled profession

WHILE VIEWING

A ▶ Watch the video. According to the video, which two of the following have contributed to fashion brand Brunello Cucinelli's success?

☐ a. its ethical employment practices   ☐ c. its investment in foreign talent

☐ b. its location in a traditional Italian village   ☐ d. its use of modern technology

B ▶ Watch the video again. Note answers to the questions below. Then discuss with a partner.

1. How does Brunello Cucinelli ensure that its staff don't work too much?

_____

_____

2. In what ways has founder Brunello Cucinelli helped the local village?

_____

_____

AFTER VIEWING

A What does Cucinelli mean when he says, "I don't think it's time wasted watching a bird in the sky when you're sewing a button"? Discuss with a partner.

B In what ways are Zara and Brunello Cucinelli similar? In what ways are they different? Note your ideas below. Then discuss with a partner.

_____

_____

Writing

EXPLORING WRITTEN ENGLISH

VOCABULARY FOR WRITING

A The following words and phrases can be useful when writing a comparative essay. Some are used to show similarities, and some are used to show differences. Put each word in the correct category.

although	both	conversely	equally
have in common	however	in contrast (to)	in the same way (that)
instead (of)	likewise	on the contrary	on the other hand
similarly	the same is true for	whereas	unlike

Similarities	Differences

LANGUAGE FOR WRITING Using Sentences with Initial Phrases

You can use initial phrases (prepositional, time, and verbal phrases) to avoid short, choppy sentences. Using initial phrases is also a way to vary your sentence style and to show the relationship between ideas. Remember to use a comma to separate the initial phrase from the main clause.

To avoid short, choppy sentences:

Samsung first started business in 1938. It was originally a trading company.

Founded in 1938, *Samsung was originally a trading company.* (verbal phrase)

To vary sentence style and/or show the relationship between ideas:

Ortega changed his store's name to Zara when he discovered that the name Zorba was already being used.

When he discovered that the name Zorba was already being used, *Ortega changed his store's name to Zara.* (time phrase)

Sergey Brin developed a search engine that would become Google in a friend's garage.

In a friend's garage, *Sergey Brin developed a search engine that would become Google.* (prepositional phrase)

B Rewrite each sentence to include an initial phrase.

1. H&M only sold women's clothing when it opened for business in 1947.

   When _____

2. Karl-Johan Persson became H&M's CEO in 2009.

   _____

3. BRS distributed shoes for a Japanese shoe maker until the spring of 1971.

   _____

4. The company's name was changed to Nike when BRS's relationship with the Japanese shoe maker ended.

   _____

   _____

WRITING SKILL Organizing a Comparative Essay

There are two main ways to organize a comparative essay: the **block method** and the **point-by-point method**.

With the **block method**, you discuss all the points of comparison about one subject and then discuss those same points about the other subject. The outline looks like this:

Introduction + Thesis statement

Body paragraph 1: Subject A

        Point 1

        Point 2

        Point 3

Body paragraph 2: Subject B

        Point 1

        Point 2

        Point 3

Conclusion

With the **point-by-point method**, you discuss each subject in terms of the points of comparison you've chosen. If there are three points of comparison, the outline looks like this:

Introduction + Thesis statement

Body paragraph 1: Point 1

        Subject A

        Subject B

Body paragraph 2: Point 2

        Subject A

        Subject B

Body paragraph 3: Point 3

        Subject A

        Subject B

Conclusion

C Look at the notes for a comparative essay on two companies. Use the notes to fill in the outline for a block comparative essay.

Notes

	Apple	Samsung
Early years	founded in Silicon Valley, United States, 1976, as tech company by S. Jobs, S. Wozniak, R. Wayne	founded in Taegu, Korea, 1938, as trading company, by Lee Byung-Chul
Marketing	direct advertising, not much social media, famous for TV ads	relies heavily on social media, celebrity endorsements, sponsorship of global events
Product development	long time to create new products, e.g. iPad	faster than Apple to assess consumer interest/marketability

OUTLINE

Organization method: ___Block_____

Notes for introduction: _Apple and Samsung are both highly successful tech companies_

_____

Thesis statement: _____

_____

Body paragraph 1:

Topic sentence: _____

Details: _____

_____

_____

Body paragraph 2:

Topic sentence: _____

Details: _____

_____

_____

Notes for conclusion: _____

_____

_____

REVISING PRACTICE

The draft on the next page is a model of the essay outlined on page 66. Follow the steps to create a better second draft.

1. Add the sentences or phrases (a–c) in the correct spaces.

   a. In contrast to Apple's direct marketing strategies,
   b. Apple Inc. is one of the largest information technology companies in the world.
   c. For example, its 2014 "Your Verse" campaign highlighted different ways people use their iPads (Beltrone, 2014).

2. Now fix the following problems (a–c) with the essay.

   a. Fix a problem with an initial phrase in paragraph B.
   b. Fix a problem with an initial phrase in paragraph C.
   c. Fix a problem with a comparison word in paragraph C.

A

From phones to tablets to TVs, Apple and Samsung products are household names around the world. In fact, both companies seem to dominate the mobile phone industry. However, while the two companies have certain features in common, they differ in terms of history, marketing styles, and the way they develop their products.

B

_____ Founded in 1976, in the heart of Silicon Valley Apple originally focused on the development and marketing of personal computers. Its founders were Steve Jobs, Steve Wozniak, and Ronald Wayne, and its early products included the Apple I, the Lisa, and the Macintosh. Today, Apple is known around the world for its well-designed phones, tablets, and other tech devices. In terms of marketing, Apple relies primarily on direct advertising and does not use social media to promote its products as much as other tech companies do. In fact, Apple is famous for its distinctive television ads. _____ Regarding product development and release, Apple usually takes quite a long time to create new products. For example, the company spent eight years developing the iPad. This reflects a key aspect of Apple's corporate culture: a determination to never release anything to the market unless it's perfect (Kaslikowski, 2013).

C

While Samsung, like Apple, is a technology company today, Samsung started out as a trading company in Taegu, Korea. Founded, in 1938 by Lee Byung-Chul, Samsung began as a grocery store, "trading and exporting goods produced in and around the city, like dried Korean fish and vegetables, as well as its own noodles" (Burris, 2017). Today, as a large conglomerate owning multiple companies, Samsung is one of the largest businesses in Korea. _____ Samsung relies heavily on social media as an avenue for advertising. The company also promotes its product with celebrity endorsements; participation in, and sponsorship of, global events; and discounts. Finally, likewise Apple spends a long time on product development, Samsung releases products in less time with the goal of assessing consumer interest and marketability. When a product is judged to be popular with consumers, then it is refined and improved.

D

Although both Apple and Samsung are leaders in the mobile phone market, their histories and strategies are distinctive. Over the years, the competitive nature of the technology industry has challenged the two companies to make each new phone more innovative than the last. Due to this, and the fact that Apple and Samsung are in intense competition with each other, it is likely the two companies will continue to create groundbreaking products far into the future.

References

Beltrone, Gabriel. (2014, Aug. 12). Apple's powerful "your verse" campaign rolls on, from Beijing and through Detroit. AdWeek. Retrieved from http://www.adweek.com/creativity/apples-powerful-your-verse-campaign-rolls-beijing-and-through-detroit-159442/.

Burris, Matthew. (2017, Sept. 7). The History of Samsung (1938-Present): Who Founded Samsung, When Samsung Was Created, and Other Facts. Lifewire. Retrieved from https://www.lifewire.com/history-of-samsung-818809.

Kaslikowski, Adam. (2013, Sept. 5). The difference between Samsung and Apple. Lucky Robot. Retrieved from http://luckyrobot.com/difference-between-samsung-and-apple/.

EDITING PRACTICE

Read the information in the box. Then find and correct one mistake with initial phrases in each sentence (1–3).

In sentences with initial phrases, remember to:
- use a comma to separate the initial phrase from the main clause
- use a prepositional, time, or verbal phrase as the initial phase

1. In 1975 Steve Wozniak, and Steve Jobs built the first Apple computer.

2. It was founded in 1949, Adidas is now one of the world's leading sports brands.

3. Offering innovative tech products Samsung is one of the most successful businesses in Korea.

UNIT REVIEW

Answer the following questions.

1. What are two ways in which Zara differs from other clothing companies?

   _____

   _____

2. What are two ways in which Brunello Cucinelli is different from Zara?

   _____

   _____

3. What are two ways to organize a comparative essay?

   _____

   _____

4. Do you remember the meanings of these words? Check (✓) the ones you know. Look back at the unit and review the ones you don't know.

   ☐ apparel
   ☐ brand
   ☐ competitive
   ☐ competitor
   ☐ executive
   ☐ found AWL
   ☐ headquarters
   ☐ marketing

   ☐ merchandise
   ☐ outsource
   ☐ profit
   ☐ retail
   ☐ rival
   ☐ shortage
   ☐ supply chain

NOTES

CITY SOLUTIONS

4

The bus rapid transit (BRT) network in Curitiba, Brazil, has inspired similar systems in other cities.

ACADEMIC SKILLS

READING Analyzing visual information
CRITICAL THINKING Analyzing quotes

THINK AND DISCUSS

1 What are the biggest cities in your country? How would you describe them?

2 What is your favorite city? What do you like about it?

A Look at the information on these pages and answer the questions.

1. What overall trends have occurred in the world's urban population since 1950?

2. Which region had the fastest percentage urban growth from 1950 to 1990? How about from 1990 to 2015?

3. Which regions are projected to urbanize fastest between now and 2050?

B Match the words in yellow to their definitions.

_____ (adj) related to a city

_____ (n) the process of increasing

_____ (adj) having a large number of people and buildings close together

AN URBAN SPECIES

Urban areas of more than a million people were rare until the early 20th century. Today, there are over 30 cities of more than 10 million people. These **dense** areas can have more than 500 inhabitants per square mile (over 195 people per square kilometer).

Growth in these high-density cities is likely to increase even more in the future as populations rise and migration from rural areas continues. In fact, two-thirds of the world's population may live in cities by 2050.

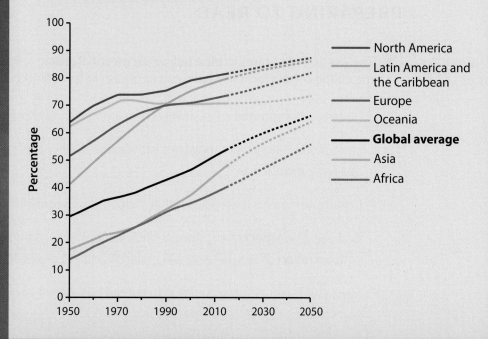

Growing Urbanization

Percentage of population living in urban areas of more than 300,000 people, 1950–2050

Legend:
- North America
- Latin America and the Caribbean
- Europe
- Oceania
- **Global average**
- Asia
- Africa

With a population of about 3 million people, Dubai is the most populous city in the United Arab Emirates.

Reading 1

PREPARING TO READ

BUILDING VOCABULARY

A The words and phrases in **blue** below are used in Reading 1. Read the sentences. Then match the correct form of each word or phrase to its definition.

> Houses in the **suburbs** are relatively cheap compared to those in the city center.
>
> Some studies show that employees with flexible working arrangements are happier and more **productive**.
>
> Many governments have policies that support low-**income** families.
>
> One negative **aspect** of city living is traffic congestion—cities **tend to** have a higher **concentration** of cars on the roads, especially during peak hours.
>
> Major cities such as Tokyo continue to **spread out** as their populations grow.

1. _____ (n) a part or side of something

2. _____ (v) to cover a huge area

3. _____ (n) money that a person earns

4. _____ (adj) able to achieve a significant amount or result

5. _____ (v) to usually do something or be a certain way

6. _____ (n) a huge amount or number of something in one place

7. _____ (n) an area outside of a large city that has homes and businesses

USING VOCABULARY

B Discuss these questions with a partner.

1. Would you rather live in a city center, a **suburb**, or a rural area? Why?

2. What **aspects** of city life appeal to you? Which aspects don't you like?

PREDICTING

C Read the title and the headings in the reading passage. What do you think the passage is mainly about? Check your idea as you read.

a. a comparison of large cities in the past and those in the present

b. the environmental challenges that growing cities are facing

c. the positive impacts of urbanization on people and the environment

LIVING ON AN
URBAN PLANET

A crowded street in
Myeongdong, Seoul

Consider this: in 1800, less than 3 percent of the world's population lived in
A cities, but by 2050, this could increase to over 66 percent. The trend is clear and
the conclusion inescapable—humans have become an urban species.

CITIES AS SOLUTIONS?

In the 19th and early 20th centuries, large urban areas began to grow and
spread. Many people viewed cities largely in negative terms—crowded, dirty,
unhealthy places full of disease and crime. People feared that as cities got
bigger, living conditions would get worse. Recent decades, however, have seen
B a widespread change in attitudes toward urbanization.[1] Many experts believe
that urbanization is good news. Although negative aspects such as pollution and
urban slums remain serious problems, many urban planners now believe big
cities might help solve the problem of Earth's growing population.

[1] **Urbanization** is the process by which cities grow.

The trading floor of the
New York Stock Exchange

importantly, Brand points out that people living in dense cities drive less. They can walk to many destinations and use public transportation. As a result, cities tend to produce fewer greenhouse gas emissions per person than suburbs.

Because of these reasons, it may be a mistake to see urbanization as evil. Instead, we should view it as an inevitable part of development, says David Satterthwaite of London's International Institute of Environment and Development. For Satterthwaite and other urban planners, rapid growth itself is not the real problem. The larger issue is how to manage the growth. There is no one model for how to manage rapid urbanization, but there are hopeful examples. One is Seoul, South Korea.

Harvard economist Edward Glaeser is one person who believes that cities bring largely positive benefits. According to Glaeser, cities are "the absence of space between people." This closeness reduces the cost of transporting goods, people, and ideas, and allows people to be more productive. Successful cities also attract and reward smart people with higher wages, and they enable people to learn from one another. According to Glaeser, a perfect example of how information can be shared in a big city is the trading floor of the New York Stock Exchange. There, employees share information in one open, crowded space. "They value knowledge over space," he says. "That's what the modern city is all about."

Another champion[2] of urbanization is environmentalist Stewart Brand. According to Brand, living in cities has a smaller impact on the environment than living in suburbs and rural areas. Cities allow half of the world's population to live on about 4 percent of the land. City roads, sewers,[3] and power lines are shorter and require fewer resources to build and operate. City apartments require less energy to heat, cool, and light than houses in other areas. Most

SEOUL'S SUCCESS STORY

Since the 1960s, Seoul's population has increased from fewer than 3 million to more than 10 million people. In the same period, South Korea has also gone from being one of the world's poorest countries to being richer than many countries in Europe. How did this happen? Large numbers of people first began arriving in Seoul in the 1950s. The government soon recognized that economic development was essential for supporting its growing urban population. It therefore began to invest in South Korean companies. This investment eventually helped corporations such as Samsung and Hyundai grow and develop. A major contributing factor for South Korea's economic success was the large number of people who came to Seoul to work.

"You can't understand urbanization in isolation from economic development," says economist Kyung-Hwan Kim of Sogang University. The growing city paid for the buildings, roads, and other infrastructure that helped absorb even more people. South Korea's growth cannot be easily copied. However, it proves that a poor country can urbanize successfully and incredibly fast.

[2] If you are a **champion** of something, you support or defend it.
[3] **Sewers** are large underground channels that carry waste matter and rainwater away.

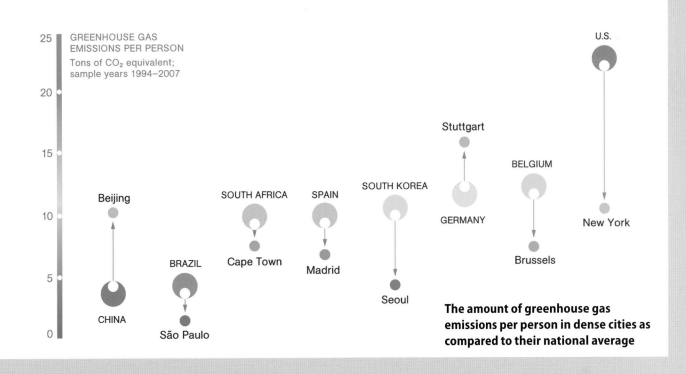

GREENHOUSE GAS EMISSIONS PER PERSON
Tons of CO_2 equivalent; sample years 1994–2007

The amount of greenhouse gas emissions per person in dense cities as compared to their national average

MANAGING URBANIZATION

H   Despite success stories such as Seoul, urban planners around the world continue to struggle with the problem of how to manage urbanization. While they used to worry mainly about city density, urban planners today are focusing on urban sprawl—the way big cities are spreading out and taking over more and more land.

I   Shlomo Angel is an urban planning professor at New York University and Princeton University. He thinks rising incomes and cheaper transportation are two main reasons for urban sprawl. "When income rises, people have money to buy more space," he says. With cheaper transportation, people can afford to travel longer distances to work. In the second half of the 20th century, for example, many people in the United States moved from cities to suburban areas. This trend led to expanding suburbs, which led to more energy use and increased air pollution and greenhouse gas emissions.

J   Today, many planners want to bring people back to downtown areas and make suburbs denser. Some ways to densify suburbs include creating walkable town centers, high-rise apartment buildings, and more public transportation. This would make people less dependent on cars. "It would be a lot better for the planet," says Edward Glaeser, if people are "in dense cities built around the elevator rather than in sprawling areas built around the car."

K   Shlomo Angel believes that planning can make a big difference in the way cities are allowed to grow. However, good planning requires looking decades ahead—reserving land for parks and public transportation, for example, before the city grows over it. It also requires looking at growing cities in a positive way, as concentrations of human energy. With the Earth's population headed toward 9 or 10 billion, dense and carefully planned cities are looking more like a solution—perhaps the best hope for lifting people out of poverty without wrecking[4] the planet.

[4] To **wreck** something means to completely destroy or ruin it.

UNDERSTANDING THE READING

SUMMARIZING **A** Read the first sentence of a summary of "Living on an Urban Planet." Check (✓) four other sentences to complete the summary.

Because most of the world's population will live in cities, it's important to plan and manage cities well so they can benefit society.

☐ 1. Urbanization has a lot of benefits, such as the easy exchange of ideas and the reduction of human impact on the environment.

☐ 2. Seoul experienced many problems as a result of its rapid population growth between 1960 and 2000.

☐ 3. Seoul's successful urbanization is an example of how urbanization can bring positive impacts to cities and countries.

☐ 4. Although some cities have managed to urbanize well, urban planners today are concerned with managing the expansion of large cities.

☐ 5. The second half of the 20th century saw many people in the United States moving out of cities.

☐ 6. Careful long-term planning is key to growing cities that can accommodate the world's future population.

UNDERSTANDING MAIN IDEAS **B** Match each section of the reading passage to its main idea.

_____ 1. Paragraph B   a. Urbanization is better for the environment.

_____ 2. Paragraph C   b. By reducing distance, cities bring largely positive benefits.

_____ 3. Paragraph D   c. Proper urban planning can bring positive results to cities.

_____ 4. Paragraphs F–G   d. Recently, attitudes toward living in cities have become more positive.

_____ 5. Paragraph J

_____ 6. Paragraph K   e. Planners want to reduce the need for cars in suburban areas.

f. Well-managed urbanization in the 20th century helped a poor country achieve rapid economic development.

IDENTIFYING PROS AND CONS **C** Answer the questions below with information from the reading passage.

1. According to Edward Glaeser, what are two benefits of living in cities? (paragraph C)

_____

2. According to Stewart Brand, what is one benefit of dense cities? What is one example he gives? (paragraph D)

_____

3. According to David Satterthwaite, what is the main challenge related to urbanization? (paragraph E)

_____

D Read the following quotes from the passage. Which main or supporting idea from the paragraph does each quote support? Discuss with a partner.

CRITICAL THINKING: ANALYZING QUOTES

1. "They value knowledge over space. That's what the modern city is all about." (paragraph C)

   _____

   _____

2. "You can't understand urbanization in isolation from economic development." (paragraph G)

   _____

   _____

3. "When income rises, people have money to buy more space." (paragraph I)

   _____

   _____

4. "It would be a lot better for the planet [if people are] in dense cities built around the elevator rather than in sprawling areas built around the car." (paragraph J)

   _____

   _____

E Do you think that city life is mainly beneficial? Why or why not? Complete the sentence below. Include at least two reasons. Then share your ideas with a partner.

CRITICAL THINKING: JUSTIFYING YOUR OPINION

Overall, I think urbanization has a **positive / negative** impact on human societies because

_____

_____

Shanghai has experienced rapid urbanization since the 1980s.

DEVELOPING READING SKILLS

When you first look at a graph, read the title, subtitle, caption, and/or legend (key). Ask yourself what information is being presented. What do the lines, colors, or symbols mean? What is the purpose of the graph? Then underline important words in the title or caption that tell you about the content. Ask yourself how the graph supports the ideas in the reading passage. How does it help you understand the author's ideas better?

ANALYZING VISUAL INFORMATION

A Work with a partner. Look at the graph below and answer the questions.

1. Look at the title, subtitle, and legend. What is the main purpose of the graph?
2. Underline the sentence in the reading passage that the graph relates to.
3. How does the graph support the sentence in the reading passage?

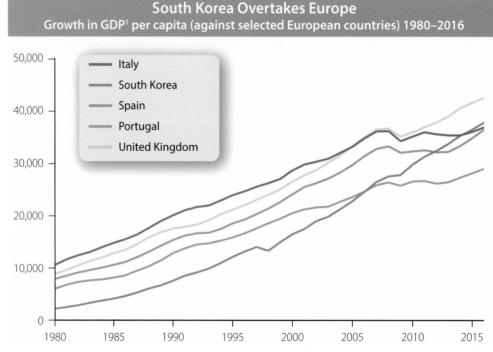

South Korea Overtakes Europe
Growth in GDP[1] per capita (against selected European countries) 1980–2016

Legend:
- Italy
- South Korea
- Spain
- Portugal
- United Kingdom

[1]**Gross Domestic Product** (GDP) is the amount of goods and services produced in one year.

ANALYZING VISUAL INFORMATION

B Look at the infographic in the reading passage and answer the questions. Discuss your answers with a partner.

1. What do the red and green colors indicate? _____
2. What is the main purpose of the chart?
   a. to show the emissions goals of certain cities and countries
   b. to show how some countries have reduced their emissions in the last 25 years
   c. to show how most cities have lower per capita emissions than their countries
3. Which paragraph in the passage does the graph support? _____

FARMING UNDERGROUND

A World War II air raid shelter in London is converted into a farm.

BEFORE VIEWING

A Read the title and the photo caption. Why do you think people would create farms underground? Discuss with a partner.

B Read the information about food miles—the distance food travels from where it's produced to people's plates—and answer the questions.

How big an impact do "food miles" have on the environment? In some parts of the world, food—such as grains, fruit, and vegetables—travels over 2,400 kilometers to get to consumers. In 2016, the United Kingdom imported about half of its food from other countries. This food is flown or shipped into the country and then transported to towns and cities in trucks. Food transportation trucks produce a quarter of transport-related greenhouse gas emissions—a major cause of global warming. And with an expanding population, these issues are only likely to increase. If producers and consumers are serious about slowing global warming, growing—and buying—more food locally could reduce "food miles."

1. How do "food miles" affect the environment?

   _____

2. Are the problems related to "food miles" likely to increase or decrease in the future? Why?

   _____

3. What do you think is one way to help reduce "food miles" where you live? Note your idea and discuss with a partner.

   _____

C The words and phrases in **bold** below are used in the video. Read the sentences. Then match the correct form of each word or phrase to its definition.

One way to be more **carbon-neutral** is to drive less and walk more.

LEDs save money and energy because they use 90 percent less power than traditional light bulbs.

The **distribution** of food by air and land can cause greenhouse gas emissions.

By **utilizing** new farming technologies—such as **hydroponic farming**—we can use fewer resources to produce the food we need.

1. _____ (n) the act of supplying goods

2. _____ (v) to use something

3. _____ (n) a device that produces light, usually used in electronics

4. _____ (adj) adding no more carbon to the atmosphere than the amount you take in

5. _____ (n) a method of growing plants in mineral-rich water

WHILE VIEWING

A ▶ Watch the video. Check (✓) the reasons Steven Dring and Richard Ballard built an underground farm.

☐ 1. to make young people aware of how food is grown

☐ 2. to grow new types of plants

☐ 3. to cut down on food miles

☐ 4. to help solve environmental problems

☐ 5. to provide food for the growing population of London

☐ 6. to use less water than traditional farming

B ▶ Watch the video again. For each statement below, circle T for true, F for false, or NG if the information is not given.

1. Steven Dring and Richard Ballard built the tunnels.	**T F NG**
2. According to Dring, the population in London will increase by two million in 10 years.	**T F NG**
3. The underground farm receives funding from the government.	**T F NG**
4. Dring and Ballard want to grow more plants in the future.	**T F NG**

AFTER VIEWING

A Steven Dring says, "We've still got kids in the U.K. who think that spaghetti is grown on trees." Why is this a problem? How can the underground farm help solve it? Discuss with a partner.

B What challenges do you think underground farms in cities might face? Think of two ideas. Then share them with a partner.

Reading 2

PREPARING TO READ

A The words in **blue** below are used in Reading 2. Complete the sentences with the correct words. Use a dictionary to help you.

attempt	basically	consumption	enhance
increasingly	industrial	majority	safety
phenomenon	varied		

1. One way to improve the _____ of city neighborhoods is to have regular police patrols.

2. According to Stewart Brand, city living actually reduces energy _____ because the _____ of people have access to public transportation and don't have to drive so much.

3. The _____ of urbanization is becoming _____ common as more and more cities continue to grow and develop.

4. Manchester used to be a(n) _____ city; from cotton to chemicals, there was a(n) _____ group of factories and businesses there.

5. Economist Edward Glaeser _____ sees cities as places where there is an absence of space between people.

6. The _____ to clean up a small river in downtown Seoul was a success—it helped _____ the attractiveness of the area.

B Discuss these questions with a partner.

USING VOCABULARY

1. What are two ways to **enhance** the quality of life in cities?

2. What can you do to reduce your energy **consumption**?

C Reading 2 is an interview with Richard Wurman, an urban planner. Wurman studied various cities to learn more about the effects of global urbanization.

PREDICTING

What kinds of information about the cities do you think he collected? Discuss with a partner. Then check your ideas as you read.

_____

_____

THE URBAN VISIONARY

A   When architect and urban planner Richard Wurman learned that the majority of Earth's population lived in cities, he became curious. He wondered what the effects of global urbanization will be. With a group of business and media partners, Wurman set out on a five-year study—a project called 19.20.21—to collect information about urbanization, focusing on the world's largest urban concentrations, or megacities.

B   The project's aim is to standardize the way information about cities—such as health, education, transportation, energy consumption, and arts and culture—is collected and shared. The hope is that urban planners will be able to use these objective data to enhance the quality of life for people in cities while reducing the environmental impact of urbanization.

Q: What draws people to cities?

C   **Wurman:** People flock to cities because of the possibilities for doing things that interest them. Those interests—and the economics that make them possible—are based on people living together. We really have turned into a world of cities. Cities cooperate with each other. Cities trade with each other. Cities are where you put museums, where you put universities, where you put the centers of government, the centers of corporations. The inventions, the discoveries, the music and art in our world all take place in these intense gatherings of individuals.

Q: Tell us about 19.20.21.

D   **Wurman:** For the first time in history, more people live in cities than outside them. I thought I'd try to discover what this new phenomenon really means. I went to the Web, and I tried to find the appropriate books and lists that would give me information, data, maps, so I could

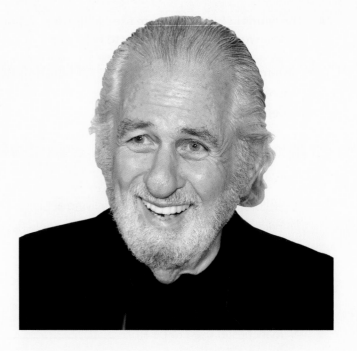

> **"**One has to understand [a city's problems] in context and in comparison to other places.**"**

understand. And I couldn't find what I was looking for. I couldn't find maps of cities to the same scale. Much of the statistical information is gathered independently by each city, and the questions they ask are often not the same. There's no readily available information on the speed of growth of cities. Diagrams on power, water distribution and quality, health care, and education aren't available, so a metropolis[1] can't find out any information about itself relative to other cities and, therefore, can't judge the success or failure of programs.

[1] A **metropolis** is a large, important, busy city.

So I decided to gather consistent information on 19 cities that will have more than 20 million people in the 21st century. That's what 19.20.21 is about. We'll have a **varied** group of young cities, old cities, third-world cities, second-world cities, first-world cities, fast-growing cities, slow-growing cities, coastal cities, inland cities, **industrial** cities, [and] cultural cities. Much of this can be presented online, but we're also planning to have exhibits and urban observatories so that cities around the world can see themselves relative to others.

Q: What are some of the cities you're looking at?

Wurman: What inspires me is being able to understand something, and understanding often comes from looking at extremes. So the cities that pop out are the ones that are clearly the largest, the oldest, the fastest-growing, the lowest, the highest, the densest, the least dense, [or] the largest in area. The densest city is Mumbai. The fastest-growing is Lagos.[2] For years, the largest city was Mexico City, but Tokyo is now the biggest … There are cities that are **basically** spread out, like Los Angeles. Then there are classic cities, which you certainly wouldn't want to leave out, like Paris. I find the data on cities to be endlessly fascinating. Just look at the world's 10 largest cities through time. The biggest city in the year 1000 was Córdoba, Spain. Beijing was the biggest city in 1500 and 1800, London in 1900, New York City in 1950, and today [it's] Tokyo.

[2]In 2017, Dhaka was the densest city, and Zinder was the fastest-growing.

Today, Plaza de la Corredera in Córdoba is a popular place for visitors to the city.

Q: Cities are increasingly challenged to sustain their infrastructure and service. Can they survive as they are now?

Wurman: Nothing survives as it is now. All cities are cities for the moment, and our thoughts about how to make them better are thoughts at the moment. There was great passion 30 years ago for the urban bulldozer,[3] that we had to tear down the slums, tear down the old parts of cities, and have urban renewal. That lasted for about 10, 15 years, until it didn't seem to work very well. And yet the reasons for doing it seemed justified at that moment … It shows that the attempt to make things better often makes things worse. We have to understand before we act. And although there are a lot of little ideas for making things better—better learning, increased safety, cleaner air—you can't solve the problem with a collection of little ideas. One has to understand them in context and in comparison to other places.

[3]A **bulldozer** is a large vehicle used for knocking down buildings.

G

THE URBAN OBSERVATORY

Wurman's team has created an interactive online exhibit called the Urban Observatory. Hoping to make the world's data "understandable and useful," the website has maps that compare different cities according to a variety of themes. These themes include the types of occupations people have, the types of transportation available, and the quality of public spaces, such as parks.

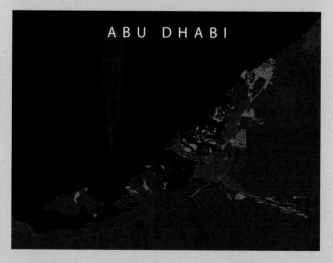

The maps above show the distribution of green spaces in three major cities.

UNDERSTANDING THE READING

A Choose the best alternative title for the reading passage.

UNDERSTANDING MAIN IDEAS

    a. An Idea for Sharing Urban Data

    b. An Idea for Improving Urban Areas

    c. An Idea for Controlling Urban Expansion

B Match each section in the passage to its purpose.

UNDERSTANDING PURPOSE

    _____ 1. Paragraph B   a. to state what the project wants to achieve

    _____ 2. Paragraph C   b. to give reasons why more people are moving to cities

    _____ 3. Paragraph D   c. to give advice on how cities should manage their development

    _____ 4. Paragraphs E–F

    _____ 5. Paragraph G   d. to describe the types of data included in the project and what they show

    e. to explain the challenges Wurman faced when studying urbanization

C Complete the concept map using information from paragraphs A, B, D, and E. Write no more than two words or a number in each space.

UNDERSTANDING DETAILS

Origins

- created by Richard Wurman, an [1]_____ and urban planner
- Wurman was curious how [2]_____ will change the world
- he set up 19.20.21 with a team of people working in [3]_____ and [4]_____
- the project was expected to last for [5]_____

Aims

- to [6]_____ the collection of city data so that it's easier to compare, e.g., all city maps use the same scale
- the data can then be used by [7]_____ to improve city living
- Wurman hopes urbanization can then have a more positive [8]_____

19.20.21

Methods

- data is collected from the world's largest cities
- study focuses on cities with populations of over [9]_____ people
- looks at how people use transportation, how much [10]_____ they consume, etc.
- information will be shared [11]_____ and via exhibits and other events

D Find the following words and phrases in the reading passage. Use context to identify their meanings. Then circle the best option to complete the definitions.

> draw (paragraph C) pop out (paragraph F)
>
> flock (paragraph C) slum (paragraph G)
>
> relative to (paragraph D)

1. Things that *draw* people to a city make them want to **go there** / **stay away**.

2. When people *flock* to a place, they go in **small** / **large** numbers.

3. *Relative to* something means **in comparison with** / **connected to** it.

4. If information *pops out*, you notice it more because it is **detailed** / **obvious**.

5. *Slums* are parts of cities where living conditions are very **poor** / **good**.

E Look at the maps in the reading passage and answer the questions below.

1. What do the maps show?

_____

2. Which city has the greatest amount? Which has the least?

_____

3. How might this information be useful for cities?

_____

_____

F Read the statements below. Which of the people in this unit—Glaeser, Brand, Angel, or Wurman—would agree most strongly with each one? Write a name for each statement. More than one answer is possible. Then share your answers with a partner.

1. Overall, people living in cities have a smaller carbon footprint. _____

2. It's better to make decisions about a city after looking at it alongside others. _____

3. Cities are efficient and important places for people to share ideas and information. _____

4. Proper planning is the way to manage urban growth and overcome problems. _____

UNIT REVIEW

Answer the following questions.

1. Why might living in cities be better than living in the suburbs? List two reasons.

   _____

   _____

   _____

2. How can a concept map help you understand a reading?

   _____

   _____

   _____

3. Do you remember the meanings of these words? Check (✓) the ones you know. Look back at the unit and review the ones you don't know.

   Reading 1:

   ☐ aspect AWL   ☐ concentration AWL   ☐ dense

   ☐ growth   ☐ income AWL   ☐ productive

   ☐ spread out   ☐ suburb   ☐ tend to

   ☐ urban

   Reading 2:

   ☐ attempt   ☐ basically   ☐ consumption AWL

   ☐ enhance AWL   ☐ increasingly   ☐ industrial

   ☐ majority AWL   ☐ phenomenon AWL   ☐ safety

   ☐ varied AWL

VOCABULARY EXTENSION   UNIT 1

Words that begin with the prefix *pre-* mean "before in time." For example, *previously* means "before the time period that you are talking about." *Pre-* can be added to some common root words. For example, *preview* means "to see a part of something before watching the whole thing."

Complete each sentence with the words below. One word is extra.

predict	prepare	preschool	prevent	preview	previous

1. It is a good idea to _____ some slides before giving a presentation.

2. Scientists are developing apps that can _____ a person's behavior better than a human can. For example, the app can tell if a customer will buy a product again.

3. For many entry-level jobs, no _____ experience is required.

4. To _____ conflict in a workplace, try to avoid aggressive behavior with your co-workers.

5. Movie companies often upload a short video online to give people a _____ of an upcoming movie and get them excited about it.

VOCABULARY EXTENSION UNIT 3

Profit and *loss* are antonyms. Below are other business words that have the opposite, or near opposite, meanings:

shortage—surplus	**cash—credit**
employer—employee	**revenue—expenditure**
supply—demand	**high-end brand—low-end brand**

A Circle the best option to complete each sentence.

1. Gucci and Armani are examples of expensive, **high-end** / **low-end** clothing brands.

2. In economic theory, an increase in **demand** / **supply** for a product usually leads to an increase in prices.

3. Many companies reinvest their **profits** / **losses** to help their business grow.

4. A company is in financial difficulty if its **expenditure** / **revenue** exceeds its **expenditure** / **revenue**.

5. A **shortage** / **surplus** of crude oil usually leads to a rise in the price drivers pay at the gas pump.

WORD FORMS Adjectives with *-ive*

Many nouns ending in *-tion* can be made into adjectives using the suffix *-ive*. The suffix *-ive* means "having the quality of." For example, *competitive* means "having the quality of competition." Here are some other examples:

action	—	*active*	*definition*	—	*definitive*
competition	—	*competitive*	*destruction*	—	*destructive*
correction	—	*corrective*	*instruction*	—	*instructive*

B Complete each sentence with one of the nouns or adjectives in the box above.

1. In economics, a monopoly is a market where there is no _____.

2. The data that financial consultants provide to a business can be very _____.

3. The rise of online shopping has been _____ to many small and medium-sized stores that struggle to compete.

4. On learning that there was a serious fault in their new product, the company needed to decide quickly upon what _____ action to take.

5. During the 2008 financial crisis, many governments took prompt _____ to stabilize the financial markets.

Below are some common expressions with the word *income*.

annual income: the amount of money you earn in a year

source of income: where you get your money from, e.g., a salary, investments, etc.

income tax: a percentage the government takes from your income in the form of taxes

disposable income: the amount of money you have left after paying taxes

income inequality: a situation where there is a difference in income levels between the highest and lowest earners

Complete each sentence with the expressions from the box above.

1. Rent from people living in property you own can be an additional _____ .

2. In the United States, the gap between top earners and low-wage earners is very large. This _____ concerns some economists.

3. If your _____ is $100,000 a year and you have to pay _____ of 20 percent, your _____ is $80,000.

WRITING REFERENCE

Initial Phrases

You can use initial phrases (prepositional, time, and verbal phrases) to avoid short, choppy sentences. Using initial phrases is also a way to vary your sentence style and to show the relationship between ideas.

Prepositional phrases	**In Africa**, Nigeria is the most populous country. **At a distance of 4.3 light-years**, Alpha Centauri is the nearest star outside our Solar System. **Just opposite this building**, you can find a really good restaurant.
Time phrases	**Since I was a young child**, I've had a keen interest in science. **When she first started the business**, there were many problems to deal with. **Once I met her**, I realized why she'd been so successful in life.
Verbal phrases	**Starting in Peru**, the Amazon River runs through seven separate countries. **Concerned about the increasing workload**, he decided to look for a new job. **Painted by Leonardo da Vinci**, the *Mona Lisa* is one of the most valuable paintings in the world.

Inversion with Negative Adverb Phrases

In formal writing, when certain negative adverb phrases are used at the start of a sentence, the subject and auxiliary verb of the main clause must be inverted (switched). Look at the examples on the right.	**Never before** <u>have I</u> found a book so difficult to put down. **Not since** I went to New Zealand <u>have I</u> seen such amazing scenery. **Not until** I arrived at the shop <u>did I</u> realize I'd forgotten my wallet.

WRITING REFERENCE

UNIT 4
Language for Writing: Using the Simple Past and the Present Perfect

Simple Past

- describes completed actions or events in the past
- often used with time expressions, e.g., *yesterday*, *last week*

> *The scientists **gave** a presentation about the research paper **last year**.*
> (The presentation was completed at a specific time in the past.)

Present Perfect

1. describes past actions or events where the specific time is unimportant or unknown

> *The scientists **have made** some interesting discoveries.*
> (The discoveries are more important than when they were made).

2. describes actions or events that happened in the past and that may continue into the future

> *The scientists **have given** several presentations about the project this year.*
> (The scientists may give more presentations before the end of the year).

3. can be used with time expressions such as *for*, *since*, and *in the* + [time period] to describe actions or events that started in the past and continue to the present

> *The project **has generated** a lot of media interest **in the past month**.*

Past Participle Forms of Commonly Used Irregular Verbs		
become—become	fall—fallen	read—read
begin—begun	find—found	say—said
bring—brought	get—gotten	see—seen
build—built	give—given	speak—spoken
buy—bought	have—had	take—taken
choose—chosen	hear—heard	tell—told
do—done	know—known	think—thought
eat—eaten	make—made	write—written

Brief Writer's Handbook

Understanding the Writing Process: The Seven Steps

The Assignment

Imagine that you have been given the following assignment: *Write an essay in which you discuss one aspect of vegetarianism.* What should you do first? What should you do second, third, and so on? There are many ways to write, but most good writers follow certain steps in the writing process. These steps are guidelines that are not always followed in order.

Look at this list of steps. Which ones do you regularly do? Which ones have you never done?

STEP 1: Choose a topic.

STEP 2: Brainstorm.

STEP 3: Outline.

STEP 4: Write the first draft.

STEP 5: Get feedback from a peer.

STEP 6: Revise the first draft.

STEP 7: Proofread the final draft.

Next, you will see how one student, Hamda, went through the steps to do the assignment. First, read the final essay that Hamda gave her teacher.

Essay 1

Better Living as a Vegetarian

1   The hamburger has become a worldwide cultural icon. Eating meat, especially beef, is an integral part of many diverse cultures. Studies show, however, that the consumption of large quantities of meat is a major contributing factor toward a great many deaths, including the unnecessarily high number of deaths from heart-related problems. Although it has caught on slowly in Western society, vegetarianism is a way of life that can help improve not only the quality of people's lives but also their longevity.

2   Surprising as it may sound, vegetarianism can have beneficial effects on the environment. Because demand for meat animals is so high, cattle are being raised in areas where rain forests once stood. As rain forest land is cleared in order to make room for cattle ranches, the environmental balance is upset; this imbalance could have serious consequences for humans. The article "Deforestation: The hidden cause of global warming" by Daniel Howden explains that much of the current global warming is due to depletion of the rain forests.

3   More important at an individual level is the question of how eating meat affects a person's health. Meat, unlike vegetables, can contain very large amounts of fat. Eating this fat has been connected—in some research cases—to certain kinds of cancer. In fact, *The St. Petersburg*

Times reports, "There was a statistically significant risk for . . . gastric cancer associated with consumption of all meat, red meat and processed meat" (Rao, 2006). If people cut down on the amounts of meat they ate, they would automatically be lowering their risks of disease. Furthermore, eating animal fat can lead to obesity, and obesity can cause numerous health problems. For example, obesity can cause people to slow down and their heart to have to work harder. This results in high blood pressure. Meat is also high in cholesterol, and this only adds to health problems. With so much fat consumption worldwide, it is no wonder that heart disease is a leading killer.

4   If people followed vegetarian diets, they would not only be healthier but also live longer. Eating certain kinds of vegetables, such as broccoli, brussels sprouts, and cauliflower, has been shown to reduce the chance of contracting colon cancer later in life. Vegetables do not contain the "bad" fats that meat does. Vegetables do not contain cholesterol, either. Furthermore, native inhabitants of areas of the world where people eat more vegetables than meat, notably certain areas of Central Asia, routinely live to be over one hundred.

5   Some people argue that, human nature being what it is, it is unhealthy for humans to not eat meat. These same individuals say that humans are naturally carnivores and cannot help wanting to consume a juicy piece of red meat. However, anthropologists have shown that early humans ate meat only when other foods were not abundant. Man is inherently a herbivore, not a carnivore.

6   Numerous scientific studies have shown the benefits of vegetarianism for people in general. There is a common thread for those people who switch from eating meat to consuming only vegetable products. Although the change of diet is difficult at first, most never regret their decision to become a vegetarian. They feel better, and those around them comment that they look better than ever before. As more and more people are becoming aware of the risks associated with meat consumption, they too will make the change.

Steps in the Writing Process
Step 1: Choose a Topic

For this assignment, the topic was given: Write an essay on vegetarianism. As you consider the assignment topic, you have to think about what kind of essay you may want to write. Will you list different types of vegetarian diets? Will you talk about the history of vegetarianism? Will you argue that vegetarianism is or is not better than eating animal products?

Hamda chose to write an argumentative essay about vegetarianism to try to convince readers of its benefits. The instructor had explained that this essay was to be serious in nature and have facts to back up the claims made.

Step 2: Brainstorm

The next step for Hamda was to brainstorm.

In this step, you write every idea about your topic that pops into your head. Some of these ideas will be good, and some will be bad; write them all. The main purpose of brainstorming is to write as many ideas as you can think of. If one idea looks especially good, you might circle that idea or put a check next to it. If you write an idea and you know right away that you are not going to use it, you can cross it out.

Brainstorming methods include making lists, clustering similar ideas, or diagramming your thoughts.

Look at Hamda's brainstorming diagram on the topic of vegetarianism.

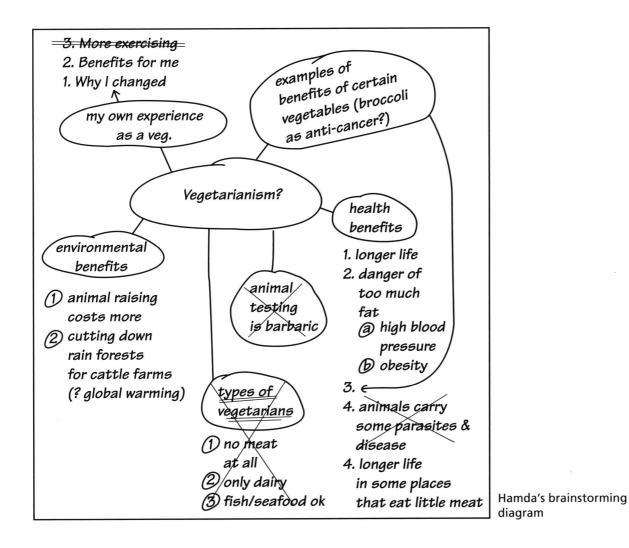

3. More exercising
2. Benefits for me
1. Why I changed

my own experience as a veg.

examples of benefits of certain vegetables (broccoli as anti-cancer?)

Vegetarianism?

health benefits

1. longer life
2. danger of too much fat
ⓐ high blood pressure
ⓑ obesity

environmental benefits

① animal raising costs more
② cutting down rain forests for cattle farms (? global warming)

animal testing is barbaric

3. ←
4. animals carry some parasites & disease
4. longer life in some places that eat little meat

types of vegetarians

① no meat at all
② only dairy
③ fish/seafood ok

Hamda's brainstorming diagram

As you can see from the brainstorming diagram, Hamda considered many aspects of vegetarianism. Notice a few items in the diagram. As she organized her brainstorming, Hamda wrote "examples of benefits of certain vegetables" as a spoke on the wheel. Then she realized that this point would be a good number three in the list of health benefits, so she drew an arrow to show that she should move it there. Since one of Hamda's brainstorming ideas (types of vegetarians) seemed to lack supporting details and was not related to her other notes, she crossed it out.

Getting the Information

How would you get the information for this brainstorming exercise?

- You might read a book or an article about vegetarianism.

- You could spend time searching online for articles on the subject.

- You could write a short questionnaire to give to classmates asking them about their personal knowledge of vegetarian practices.

- You could also interview an expert on the topic, such as a nutritionist.

Writer's Note

Doing Research

To get a deeper understanding of your essay topic, you may choose to do some research. Remember that any information you get from an outside source needs to be credited in your essay. Writers do NOT use others' ideas in their writing without giving the proper credit.

Take another look at Hamda's essay. Can you find the places where she used outside sources to back up her ideas?

Step 3: Outline

Next, create an outline for the essay. Here is Hamda's rough outline that she wrote from her brainstorming notes.

I.   Introduction
   A. Define vegetarianism
   B. List different types
   C. Thesis statement

II. Environmental benefits (Find sources to support!)
   A. Rain forests
   B. Global warming

III. Health issues (Find sources to support!)
   A. Too much fat from meat → obesity → diseases → cancer
   B. High blood pressure and heart disease
   C. Cancer-fighting properties of broccoli and cauliflower, etc.

IV. Counterargument and refutation
   A. Counterargument: Man is carnivore.
   B. Refutation

V.   Conclusion
   A. Restate thesis
   B. Opinion: Life will improve.

Supporting Details

After you have chosen the main points for your essay you will need to develop some supporting details. You should include examples, reasons, explanations, definitions, or personal experiences. In some cases, such as this argumentative essay on vegetarianism, it is a good idea to include outside sources or expert opinions that back up your claims.

One common technique for generating supporting details is to ask specific questions about the topic, for example:

What is it?

What happened?

How did this happen?

What is it like or not like? Why?

Step 4: Write the First Draft

Next, Hamda wrote her first draft. As she wrote each paragraph of the essay, she paid careful attention to the language she used. She chose a formal sentence structure including a variety of sentence types. In addition, her sentences varied in length, with the average sentence containing almost 20 words. (Sentences in conversation tend to be very short; sentences in academic writing tend to be longer.) Hamda also took great care in choosing appropriate vocabulary. In addition to specific terminology, such as *obesity, blood pressure,* and *consumption*, she avoided the conversational *you* in the essay, instead referring to *people* and *individuals*.

In this step, you use information from your brainstorming session and outline to write the essay. This first draft may contain many errors, such as misspellings, incomplete ideas, and comma errors. At this point, you should not worry about correcting the errors. The main thing is to put your ideas into sentences.

You may feel that you do not know what you think about the topic yet. In this case, it may be difficult for you to write, but it is important to just write, no matter what comes out. Sometimes writing helps you think, and as soon as you form a new thought, you can write it.

Better Living as a Vegetarian

Wow — too abrupt? You don't talk about hamburgers anymore??

(Do you like hamburgers?) Eating meat, especially beef, is an ~~interesting~~ part of the
vocabulary?

daily life around the world. In addition, this high (eating) of meat is a major contributing
word choice?

factor ~~thing~~ *causes* that makes a great many deaths, including the unnecessarily high number of

deaths from heart-related problems. Vegetarianism has caught on slowly in some parts

, and it
of the world. ~~Vegetarianism~~ is a way of life that can help improve not only the quality of

people's lives but also people's longevity. → *the quality but also the length of people's lives*

This is not a topic sentence
   Because demand for meat animals is (so high.) Cattle are being raised in areas where
                                                    c

the rainforest once stood. As rain forest land is cleared in massive amounts in order to

make room for the cattle ranches, the environmental balance is being upset. This could

For example,   *transition?*
have serious consequences for us in both the near and long term. How much of the current

global warming is due to man's disturbing the rain forest?

You need a more specific topic relating to health.
(Meat contains a high amount of fat.) Eating this fat has been connected in research

cases with certain kinds of cancer. Furthermore, eating animal fat can lead to obesity, and

obesity can cause many different kinds of diseases, for example, obesity can cause people

to slow down and their heart to have to word harder. This results in high blood pressure.

   Meat is high in cholesterol, and this only adds to the health problems. With the high

consumption of animal fat by so many people, it is no wonder that heart disease is a

leading killer.

Hamda's first draft

On the other hand, eating a vegetarian diet can improve a person's health. And

necessary?

vegetables taste so good. In fact, it can even save someone's life. Eating certain kinds

of vegetables, such as broccoli, brussels sprouts, and cauliflower, has been shown to

reduce the chance of having colon cancer later in life. Vegetables do not contain

combine sentences?

the "bad" fats that meat does. Vegetables do not contain cholesterol, either. Native

inhabitants of areas of the world where mostly vegetables are consumed, notably

certain areas of the former Soviet republics, routinely live to be over one hundred.

good sentence

Although numerous scientific studies have shown the benefits of vegetarianism for people

in general, I know firsthand how my life has improved since I decided to give up meat entirely.

In 2006, I saw a TV program that discussed problems connected to animals that are raised for

food. The program showed how millions of chickens are raised in dirty, crowded conditions

not related to your topic

until they are killed. The program also talked about how diseases can be spread from cow or

pig to humans due to unsanitary conditions. Shortly after I saw this show, I decided to try life

without eating meat. Although it was difficult at first, I have never regretted my decision to

become a vegetarian. I feel better and my friends tell me that I look better than ever before.

Being a vegetarian has many benefits. Try it.

*This is too short!
How about making a
prediction or suggestion
for the reader? The previous
paragraph told how the writer
became a vegetarian, so
doesn't it make sense for the
conclusion to say something
like "I'm sure your life will
be better too if you become a
vegetarian"?*

*I like this essay.
You really need to
work on
the conclusion.*

Making Changes

As you write the first draft, you may want to add information or take some out. In some cases, your first draft may not follow your outline exactly. That is OK. Writers do not always stick with their original plan or follow the steps in the writing process in order. Sometimes they go back and forth between steps. The writing process is much more like a cycle than a line.

Reread Hamda's first draft with her teacher's comments.

First Draft Tips

Here are some things to remember about the first draft copy:

- The first draft is not the final copy. Even native speakers who are good writers do not write an essay only one time. They rewrite as many times as necessary until the essay is the best that it can be.

- It is OK for you to make notes on your drafts; you can circle words, draw connecting lines, cross out words, or write new information. Make notes to yourself about what to change, what to add, or what to reconsider.

- If you cannot think of a word or an idea as you write, leave a blank space or circle. Then go back and fill in the space later. If you write a word that you know is not the right one, circle or underline it so you can fill in the right word later. Do not stop writing. When people read your draft, they can see these areas you are having trouble with and offer comments that may help.

- Do not be afraid to throw some sentences away if they do not sound right. Just as a good housekeeper throws away unnecessary things from the house, a good writer throws out unnecessary or wrong words or sentences.

The handwriting in the first draft is usually not neat. Sometimes it is so messy that only the writer can read it! Use a word-processing program, if possible, to make writing and revising easier.

Step 5: Get Feedback from a Peer

Hamda used Peer Editing Sheet 8 to get feedback on her essay draft. Peer editing is important in the writing process. You do not always see your own mistakes or places where information is missing because you are too close to the essay that you created. Ask someone to read your draft and give you feedback about your writing. Choose someone that you trust and feel comfortable with. While some people feel uneasy about peer editing, the result is almost always a better essay. Remember to be polite when you edit another student's paper.

Step 6: Revise the First Draft

This step consists of three parts:

1. React to the comments on the peer editing sheet.

2. Reread the essay and make changes.

3. Rewrite the essay one more time.

Step 7: Proofread the Final Draft

Most of the hard work is over now. In this step, the writer pretends to be a brand-new reader who has never seen the essay before. Proofread your essay for grammar, punctuation, and spelling errors and to see if the sentences flow smoothly.

Read Hamda's final paper again on pages 95–96.

Of course, the very last step is to turn the paper in to your teacher and hope that you get a good grade!

Writer's Note

Proofreading

One good way to proofread your essay is to set it aside for several hours or a day or two. The next time you read your essay, your head will be clearer and you will be more likely to see any problems. In fact, you will read the composition as another person would.

Editing Your Writing

While you must be comfortable writing quickly, you also need to be comfortable with improving your work. Writing an assignment is never a one-step process. For even the most gifted writers, it is often a multiple-step process. When you were completing your assignments in this book, you probably made some changes to your work to make it better. However, you may not have fixed all of the errors. The paper that you turned in to your teacher is called a first draft, which is sometimes referred to as a rough draft.

A first draft can often be improved. One way to improve an essay is to ask a classmate, friend, or teacher to read it and make suggestions. Your reader may discover that one of your paragraphs is missing a topic sentence, that you have made grammar mistakes, or that your essay needs better vocabulary choices. You may not always like or agree with the comments from a reader, but being open to changes will make you a better writer.

This section will help you become more familiar with how to identify and correct errors in your writing.

Step 1

Below is a student's first draft for a timed writing. The writing prompt for this assignment was "For most people, quitting a job is a very difficult decision. Why do people quit their jobs?" As you read the first draft, look for areas that need improvement and write your comments. For example, does the writer use the correct verb tenses? Is the punctuation correct? Is the vocabulary suitable for the intended audience? Does the essay have an appropriate hook?

There Are Many Reasons Why People Quit Their Jobs

Joann quit her high-paying job last week. She had had enough of her coworkers' abuse. Every day they would make fun of her and talk about her behind her back. Joann's work environment was too stressful, so she quit. Many employees quit their jobs. In fact, there are numerous reasons for this phenomenon.

First, the job does not fit the worker. Job seekers may accept a job without considering their skills. Is especially true when the economy is slowing and jobs are hard to find. The workers may try their best to change themselves depending on the work. However, at some point they realize that they are not cut out in this line of work and end up quitting. This lack of understanding or ability make people feel uncomfortable in their jobs. So they begin to look for other work.

Another reason people quit their jobs is the money. Why do people work in the first place? They work in order to make money. If employees are underpaid, he cannot earn enough to support himself or his family. The notion of working, earning a decent salary, and enjoy life is no longer possible. In this case, low-paid workers have no choice but to quit their jobs and search for a better-paying position.

Perhaps the biggest situation that leads people to quit their jobs is personality conflicts. It is really difficult for an employee to wake up every morning, knowing that they will be spending the next eight or nine hours in a dysfunctional environment. The problem can be with bosses or coworkers but the result is the same. Imagine working for a discriminate boss or colleagues which spread rumors. The stress levels increases until that employee cannot stand the idea of going to work. The employee quits his or her job in the hope of finding a more calm atmosphere somewhere else.

Work should not be a form of punishment. For those people who have problems with not feeling comfortable on the job, not getting paid enough, and not respected, it *does* feel like punishment. As a result, they quit and continue their search for a job that will give them a sense of pride, safety, and friends.

Step 2

Read the teacher's comments on the first draft of "There Are Many Reasons Why People Quit Their Jobs." Are these the same things that you noticed?

The title should NOT be a complete sentence.

There Are Many Reasons Why People Quit Their Jobs

Consider changing your hook/introduction. The introduction here is already explaining one of the reasons for quitting a job. This information should be in the body of the essay. Suggestion: Use a "historical" hook describing how people were more connected to their jobs in the past than they are now.

Joann quit her high-paying job last week. She had had enough of her coworkers' abuse. Every day they would make fun of her and talk about her behind her back. Joann's work environment was too stressful, so she quit. Many employees quit their jobs. In fact, there are numerous reasons for this phenomenon.

Try to use another transition phrase instead of first, second, etc.

add transition

(First,) the job does not fit the worker. ⌄Job seekers may accept a job without considering their

word choice—be more specific   fragment

(skills.) Is especially true when the economy is slowing and jobs are hard to find. The workers may

word choice—better: "adapt to"

try their best to (change themselves depending on) the work. However, at some point they realize

prep

that they are not cut out (in) this line of work and end up quitting. This lack of understanding or

S-V agreement   fragment

ability (make) people feel uncomfortable in their (jobs. So) they begin to look for other work.

word choice—be more specific

Another reason people quit their jobs is the (money.) Why do people work in the first place?

They work in order to make money. If (employees) are underpaid, (he) cannot earn enough to

pronoun agreement

// not parallel—use "-ing"

support (himself) or (his family.) The notion of working, earning a decent salary, and (enjoy) life is

word choice   Do you mean "underpaid"?

no longer (possible.) In this case, (low-paid) workers have no choice but to quit their jobs and

search for a better-paying position.

word choice—too vague

Perhaps the (biggest) situation that leads people to quit their jobs is personality conflicts. It is

word choice—avoid using "really"   *pronoun agreement*

(really) difficult for an employee to wake up every morning, knowing that (they) will be spending

add another descriptive word here   *word choice—too vague*

the next eight or nine hours in a dysfunctional ^ environment. The (problem) can be with bosses

punc. (add comma)   *word choice*

or coworkers but the result is the same. Imagine working for a (discriminate) boss or colleagues

word form   *S-V agreement*   *write it out—better: "can no longer"*

(which) spread rumors. The stress levels (increases) until that employee (can't) stand the idea of

add transition   *word choice—better: "serene"*

going to work. ^ The employee quits his or her job in the hope of finding a more (calm) atmosphere

somewhere else.

thought of as   *word choice*

Work should not be ^ a form of punishment. For those people who (have problems) with not

// not parallel—use "-ing"

feeling comfortable on the job, not getting paid enough, and (not respected,) it *does* feel like

punishment. As a result, they quit and continue their search for a job that will give them a

word choice—better: "camaraderie"

sense of pride, safety, and (friends.)

Step 3

Now read the second draft of this essay. How is it the same as the first draft? How is it different? Did the writer fix all the sentence mistakes?

Two Weeks' Notice

A generation ago, it was common for workers to stay at their place of employment for years and years. When it was time for these employees to retire, companies would offer a generous pension package and, sometimes, a token of appreciation, such as a watch, keychain, or other trinket. Oh, how times have changed. Nowadays, people—especially younger workers—jump from job to job like bees fly from flower to flower to pollinate. Some observers might say that today's workforce is not as serious as yesterday's. This is too simple an explanation, however. In today's society, fueled by globalization, recession, and other challenges, people quit their jobs for a number of valid reasons.

One reason for quitting a job is that the job does not fit the worker. In other words, job seekers may accept a job without considering their aptitude for it. This is especially true when the economy is slowing and jobs are hard to find. The workers may try their best to adapt themselves to the work. However, at some point they realize that they are not cut out for this line of work and end up quitting. This lack of understanding or ability makes people feel uncomfortable in their jobs, so they begin to look for other work.

Another reason people quit their jobs is the salary. Why do people work in the first place? They work in order to make money. If employees are underpaid, they cannot earn enough to support themselves or their families. The notion of working, earning a decent salary, and enjoying life is no longer viable. In this case, underpaid workers have no choice but to quit their jobs and search for a better-paying position.

Perhaps the most discouraging situation that leads people to quit their jobs is personality conflicts. It is extremely difficult for an employee to wake up every morning knowing that he or she will be spending the next eight or nine hours in a dysfunctional and often destructive environment. The discord can be with bosses or coworkers, but the result is the same. Imagine working for a bigoted boss or colleagues who spread rumors. The stress levels increase until that employee can no longer stand the idea of going to work. In the end, the employee quits his or her job with the hope of finding a more serene atmosphere somewhere else.

Work should not be thought of as a form of punishment. For those people who struggle with not feeling comfortable on the job, not getting paid enough, and not being respected, it *does* feel like punishment. As a result, they quit and continue their search for a job that will give them a sense of pride, safety, and camaraderie.

Sentence Types

English sentence structure includes three basic types of sentences: simple, compound, and complex. These labels indicate how the information in a sentence is organized, not how difficult the content is.

Simple Sentences

1. Simple sentences usually contain one subject and one verb.

> S V
> |Kids| love television.

> V S V
> Does |this| sound like a normal routine?

2. Sometimes simple sentences can contain more than one subject or verb.

> S V
> |Brazil and the United States| are large countries.

> S V V
> |Brazil| lies in South America and has a large population.

> S V V
> |We| traveled throughout Brazil and ended our trip in Argentina.

Compound Sentences

Compound sentences are usually made up of two simple sentences (independent clauses). Compound sentences need a coordinating conjunction (connector) to combine the two sentences. The coordinating conjunctions include:

> for   and   nor   but   or   yet   so

Many writers remember these conjunctions with the acronym *FANBOYS*. Each letter represents one conjunction: *F = for, A = and, N = nor, B = but, O = or, Y = yet,* and *S = so.*

Remember that a comma is always used before a coordinating conjunction that separates the two independent clauses.

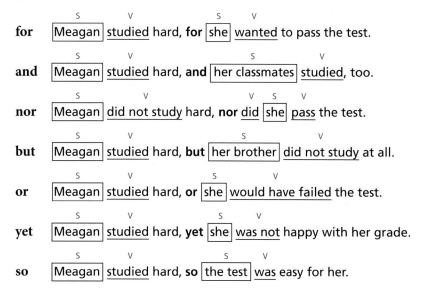

Study the following examples of compound sentences. Draw a |box| around each subject, underline each verb, and (circle) each coordinating conjunction.

1. Brazil was colonized by Europeans, and its culture has been greatly influenced by this fact.

2. This was my first visit to the international section of the airport, and nothing was familiar.

3. Many people today are overweight, and being overweight has been connected to some kinds of cancer.

4. Barriers fell, markets opened, and people rejoiced in the streets because they anticipated a new life full of opportunities and freedom to make their own choices.

5. Should public school students make their own individual decisions about clothing, or should all students wear uniforms?

6. This question has been asked many times, but people are not in agreement about the ultimate punishment.

Complex Sentences

Like compound sentences, complex sentences are made up of two parts. Complex sentences, however, contain one independent clause and, at least, one dependent clause. In most complex sentences, the dependent clause is an adverb clause.

Complex Sentences (with Adverb Clauses)

Adverb clauses begin with subordinating conjunctions, which include the following:

while   although   after   because   if   before

Study the examples below. The adverb clauses are underlined, and the subordinating conjunctions are boldfaced.

The hurricane struck **while** we were at the mall.

After the president gave his speech, he answered most of the reporters' questions.

Unlike coordinating conjunctions, which join two independent clauses but are not part of either clause, subordinating conjunctions are actually part of the dependent clause.

Joe played tennis   **after** Vicky watched TV.

independent clause   dependent clause

The subordinating conjunction *after* does not connect the clauses *Joe played tennis* and *Vicky watched TV*; *after* is grammatically part of *Vicky watched TV*.

Remember that dependent clauses must be attached to an independent clause. They cannot stand alone as a sentence. If they are not attached to another sentence, they are called fragments, or incomplete sentences. Fragments are incomplete ideas, and they cause confusion for the reader. In a complex sentence, both clauses are needed to make a complete idea so the reader can understand what you mean. Look at these examples:

Fragment:	After Vicky watched TV
Complete Sentence:	Joe played tennis after Vicky watched TV.
	or
Complete Sentence:	After Vicky watched TV, she went to bed.

Study the following examples of complex sentences from the essays in this book. Draw a ☐box☐ around each subject, <u>underline</u> each verb, and (circle) each subordinating conjunction.

1. While the Northeast is experiencing snowstorms, cities like Miami, Florida, can have temperatures over 80 degrees Fahrenheit.

2. Although Brazil and the United States are unique countries, there are remarkable similarities in their size, ethnic diversity, and personal values.

3. Another bus arrived at the terminal, and the passengers stepped off carrying all sorts of luggage.

4. While it is true that everyone makes a blunder from time to time, some people do not have the courage to admit their errors because they fear blame.

5. Because almost every area has a community college, students who opt to go to a community college first can continue to be near their families for two more years.

Additional Grammar Activities

The three example essays in this section feature different grammatical errors. Each paragraph highlights one kind of error. In each case, read the entire essay before you complete the activities.

Before you complete Activities 1–5, read the whole essay first. Then go back and complete each activity.

ACTIVITY 1 Verb Forms

Read the paragraph and decide whether the five underlined verbs are correct. If not, draw a line through the verb and write the correct form above the verb.

Essay 2

A Simple Recipe

1   "When in Rome, do as the Romans do" may <u>sound</u> ridiculous, but this proverb <u>offer</u> an important suggestion. If you travel to other countries, especially to a country that is very different from your own, you should <u>keeping</u> this saying in mind. For example, Japan has unique customs that <u>is</u> not found in any other country. If you <u>traveled</u> to Japan, you should find out about Japanese customs, taboos, and people beforehand.

ACTIVITY 2 Verb Forms

Read this paragraph carefully. Then write the correct form of the verbs in parentheses.

2   One custom is that you should (take) _____ off your shoes before (enter) _____ someone's house. In Japan, the floor must always be kept clean because usually people (sit) _____, eat a meal, or even (sleep) _____ on the floor. Another custom

is giving gifts. The Japanese often (give) _____ a small gift
to people who have (do) _____ favors for them. Usually this
token of gratitude (give) _____ in July and December to keep
harmonious relations with the receiver. When you (give) _____
someone such a gift, you should make some form of apology about it. For
example, many Japanese will say, "This is just a small gift that I have for you."
In addition, it is not polite to open a gift immediately. The receiver usually
(wait) _____ until the giver has left so the giver will not be
embarrassed if the gift (turn) _____ out to be defective or
displeasing.

ACTIVITY 3 **Connectors**

Read the paragraph carefully. Then fill in the blanks with one of these connectors:

because   in addition   even if   for example   first   but

3 _____, it is important to know about Japanese
taboos. All cultures have certain actions that are considered socially
unacceptable. _____ something is acceptable in one culture,
it can easily be taboo in another culture. _____, chopsticks
are used in many cultures, _____ there are two taboos about
chopsticks etiquette in Japan. _____, you should never stand
the chopsticks upright in your bowl of rice. _____ standing
chopsticks upright is done at a funeral ceremony, this action is associated
with death. Second, you must never pass food from one pair of chopsticks
to another. Again, this is related to burial rites in Japan.

ACTIVITY 4 **Articles**

There are 14 blanks in this paragraph. Read the paragraph and write the articles *a, an,* or *the* to
complete the sentences. Some blanks do not require articles.

4 Third, it is important to know that Japanese people have
_____ different cultural values. One of _____
important differences in _____ cultural values is
_____ Japanese desire to maintain _____
harmony at all costs. People try to avoid causing any kind of dispute.
If there is _____ problem, both sides are expected to
compromise in order to avoid an argument. People are expected to
restrain their emotions and put _____ goal of compromise
above their individual wishes. Related to this is _____
concept of patience. Japanese put _____ great deal of

_____ value on _____ patience. Patience also contributes to maintaining _____ good relations with _____ everyone and avoiding _____ disputes.

ACTIVITY 5 **Prepositions**

Read this paragraph and write the correct preposition in each blank. Choose from these prepositions: *into, in, to, about, with, of,* and *around*. You may use them more than once.

5 _____ conclusion, if you want to get along well

_____ the Japanese and avoid uncomfortable situations

when you go _____ Japan, it is important to take

_____ account the features _____ Japanese

culture that have been discussed here. Although it may be hard to

understand Japanese customs because they are different, knowing

_____ them can help you adjust to life in Japan. If you face

an unfamiliar or difficult situation when you are _____

Japan, you should do what the people _____ you do. In other

words, "When _____ Japan, do as the Japanese do."

Before you complete Activities 6–12, read the whole essay. Then go back and complete each activity.

ACTIVITY 6 **Verb Forms**

Read this paragraph carefully. Then write the correct form of the verbs in parentheses.

Essay 3

Dangers of Corporal Punishment

1 What should parents do when their five-year-old child says
a bad word even though the child knows it is wrong? What should a
teacher (do) _____ when a student in the second grade
(call) _____ the teacher a name? When my parents (be)
_____ children forty or fifty years ago, the answer to these
questions was quite clear. The adult would spank the child immediately.
Corporal punishment (be) _____ quite common then. When
I was a child, I (be) _____ in a class in which the teacher got
angry at a boy who kept (talk) _____ after she told him to
be quiet. The teacher then (shout) _____ at the boy and, in

front of all of us, (slap) _____ his face. My classmates and
I were shocked. Even after twenty years, I still remember that incident
quite clearly. If the teacher's purpose (be) _____ to (teach)
_____ us to (be) _____ quiet, she did not
(succeed) _____. However, if her purpose was to create an
oppressive mood in the class, she succeeded. Because corporal punishment
(be) _____ an ineffective and cruel method of discipline, it
should never be (use) _____ under any circumstances.

ACTIVITY 7 **Prepositions**

Read this paragraph carefully. Write the correct preposition in each blank. Use these prepositions: *in,*
of, and *for*.

2   Supporters _____ corporal punishment claim that
physical discipline is necessary _____ developing a child's
sense _____ personal responsibility. Justice Lewis Powell, a
former U.S. Supreme Court justice, has even said that paddling children
who misbehave has been an acceptable method _____
promoting good behavior and responsibility _____ school
children for a long time. Some people worry that stopping corporal
punishment in schools could result _____ a decline
_____ school achievement. However, just because a student
stops misbehaving does not mean that he or she suddenly has a better
sense _____ personal responsibility or correct behavior.

ACTIVITY 8 **Articles**

Read the paragraph and write the articles *a, an,* or *the* to complete the sentences. Some blanks do not
require articles.

3   Corporal punishment is _____ ineffective way
to punish _____ child because it may stop a behavior
for a while, but it will not necessarily have _____
long-term effect. Thus, if an adult inflicts _____ mild
form of _____ corporal punishment that hurts the child
very little or not at all, it will not get rid of the bad behavior. Moreover,
because corporal punishment works only temporarily, it will have
to be repeated whenever the child misbehaves. It may then become
_____ standard response to any misbehavior. This can lead
to _____ frequent and more severe spanking, which may
result in _____ abuse.

ACTIVITY 9 **Comma Splices**

Read this paragraph carefully and find the two comma splices. Correct them in one of two ways: (1) change the comma to a period and make two sentences or (2) add a connector after the comma.

4   A negative effect of corporal punishment in school is that it makes some students feel aggressive toward parents, teachers, and fellow students. In my opinion, children regard corporal punishment as a form of teacher aggression that makes them feel helpless. Therefore, students may get frustrated if corporal punishment is used frequently. Furthermore, it increases disruptive behavior that can become more aggressive, this leads to school violence and bullying of fellow students. Supporters of corporal punishment believe that it is necessary to maintain a good learning environment, it is unfortunate that the opposite result often happens. The learning environment actually becomes less effective when there is aggressive behavior.

ACTIVITY 10 **Verb Forms**

Read the paragraph and decide whether the underlined verbs are correct. If not, draw a line through the verb and write the correct form above it.

5   Last, corporal punishment may <u>result</u> in antisocial behavior later in life because it teaches children that adults <u>condone</u> violence as a solution to problems. Children who are <u>spank</u> learn that it is acceptable for a stronger person <u>using</u> violence against a weaker person. The concept of "might makes right" is <u>forced</u> upon them at a very early age. Furthermore, this concept teaches a lesson not only to those who are spanked but also to those who <u>witness</u> it. Studies of prisoners and delinquents <u>shows</u> that nearly 100 percent of the violent inmates at San Quentin and 64 percent of juvenile delinquents <u>was</u> victims of seriously abusive punishment during childhood. If serious punishment <u>causes</u> antisocial behavior, perhaps even milder punishment also <u>contribute</u> to violence. Research at the University of New Hampshire <u>will find</u> that children who were spanked between the ages of three and five <u>showed</u> higher levels of antisocial behavior when they <u>were observed</u> just two and four years later. This behavior included higher levels of beating family members, hitting fellow students, and defying parents. It is ironic that the behaviors for which teachers <u>punishing</u> students often get worse as a result of the spanking.

ACTIVITY 11 Editing for Errors

There are seven errors in this paragraph. They are in word forms (two), articles (one), sentence fragments (one), verb tense (one), and subject-verb agreement (two). Mark these errors and write corrections.

6   For punishment to be effective, it must produce a great behavioral change, result in behavior that is permanent, and produce minimal side effects. However, none of these changes is a result of corporal punishment. Therefore, we should consider alternatives to corporal punishment. Because discipline is necessary to educate children. One of the alternatives are to emphasize students' positive behaviors. Some research shows that reward, praise, and self-esteem is the most powerful motivators for the learning. Other alternatives are to hold conferences with students to help them plan acceptable behave or to use school staff, such as psychologists and counselors. It is important to build better interpersonal relations between teachers and students. In addition to these alternatives, instruction that reaches all students, such as detention, in-school suspension, and Saturday school, is available to discipline and punishment unruly students, too. Alternatives to corporal punishment taught children to be self-disciplined rather than to be cooperative only because of fear.

ACTIVITY 12 Editing for Errors

There are seven errors in this paragraph. They are in word forms (one), articles (three), sentence fragments (one), comma splices (one), and subject-verb agreement (one). Mark these errors and write the corrections.

7   In the conclusion, teachers should not use corporal punishment because it is ineffective in disciplining students and may have long-term negative effects on students. Moreover, teachers should not forget that love and understanding must be part of any kind of discipline. Discipline and love is not opposites, punishment must involve letting the children know that what they do is wrong and why punishment is necessary. Teachers should not just beat student with the hopeful that he will understand. It is important to maintain discipline without inflicting physical pain on students. Therefore, teachers should use effective and more humane alternatives. In order to bring about permanent behavioral changes.

Before you complete Activities 13–18, read the whole essay. Then go back and complete each activity.

ACTIVITY 13 Articles

Read the paragraph and write the articles *a, an,* or *the* to complete the sentences. Some blanks do not require articles.

Washington and Lincoln

1   Perhaps no other names from _____ American history are better known than the names of George Washington and Abraham Lincoln. Both of these presidents made valuable contributions to _____ United States during their presidency. In fact, one could argue that _____ America would not be _____ same country that it is today if either of these two leaders had not been involved in _____ American politics. However, it is interesting to note that although both leaders made _____ significant contributions to _____ country, they lived in _____ quite different times and served in _____ very different ways.

ACTIVITY 14 Verb Forms

Read this paragraph carefully. Then write the correct form of the verbs in parentheses.

2   Everyone (know) _____ that George Washington was the first president of the United States. What most people do not (appreciate) _____ (be) _____ that Washington (be) _____ a clever military leader. He served the country in the early days of the Revolution by (help) _____ to change the colonial volunteers from ragged farmers into effective soldiers. Without Washington's bravery and military strategy, it is doubtful that the colonies could have (beat) _____ the British. Thus, without Washington, the colonies might never even have (become) _____ the United States of America.

ACTIVITY 15　Prepositions

Read this paragraph and write the correct preposition in each blank. Choose from these prepositions: *from, in, to, with, for, between,* and *of.* You may use them more than once.

3　　　Abraham Lincoln was the sixteenth president _____ the United States. He was elected president _____ 1860 during a controversial and heated period of American history. As more states applied _____ membership in the growing country, the issue _____ slavery kept surfacing. There was an unstable balance _____ slave states and free states. Each time another state was added _____ the Union, the balance of power shifted. Lincoln was _____ a free state, and many _____ the slave state leaders viewed Lincoln as an enemy of their cause _____ expand slavery. _____ the end, no compromise could be reached, and the slave states seceded _____ the United States in order to form their own independent country. Hostilities grew, and _____ 1861 the Civil War, or the War _____ the States as it is sometimes called, broke out. During the next four years, the Civil War ravaged the country. By the end of the war in 1865, the American countryside was _____ shambles, but the Union was once again intact. Through his military and political decisions, Lincoln is credited _____ saving the country _____ self-destruction.

ACTIVITY 16　Editing for Errors

There are eight errors in this paragraph. They are in word forms (one), articles (two), modals (one), verb tense (two), and subject-verb agreement (two). Mark these errors and write corrections.

4　　　Washington and Lincoln was similarly in several ways. Both men are U.S. presidents. Both men served the United States during extremely difficult times. For Washington, the question is whether the United States would be able to maintain its independence from Britain. The United States was certainly very fragile nation at that time. For Lincoln, the question were really not so different. Would the United States to be able to survive during what was one of darkest periods of American history?

ACTIVITY 17 Sentence Fragments

After you read this paragraph, find the three sentence fragments. Correct the fragments by (1) changing the punctuation and creating one complete sentence or (2) adding new words to make the fragment a complete sentence.

5   There were also several differences between Washington and Lincoln. Washington came from a wealthy aristocratic background. He had several years of schooling. Lincoln came from a poor background, and he had very little schooling. Another difference between the two involved their military roles. Washington was a general. He was a military leader. Became president. Lincoln never served in the military. He was a lawyer who early on became a politician. When he became president, he took on the role of commander in chief, as all U.S. presidents do. Despite his lack of military background or training. Lincoln made several strategic decisions that enabled the U.S. military leaders to win the Civil War. Finally, Washington served for two terms and therefore had eight years to accomplish his policies. Lincoln, on the other hand, was assassinated. While in office and was not able to finish some of the things that he wanted for the country.

ACTIVITY 18 Editing for Errors

There are seven errors in this paragraph. They are in articles (two), verb tense (one), inappropriate words (one), word forms (one), number (singular and plural) (one), and subject-verb agreement (one). Mark these errors and make corrections.

6   The names George Washington and Abraham Lincoln is known even to people who have never been to the United States. Both of these patriots gave large part of their lives to help America make what it is today though they served the country in very different ways in complete different time in the American history. Although they were gone, their legacies and contributions continue to have an impact on our lives.

Connectors

Using connectors will help your ideas flow. Remember that when connectors occur at the beginning of a sentence, they are often followed by a comma.

Purpose	Coordinating Conjunctions (connect independent clauses)	Subordinating Conjunctions (begin dependent clauses)	Transitions (usually precede independent clauses)
Examples			For example, To illustrate, Specifically, In particular,
Information	and		In addition, Moreover, Furthermore,
Comparison			Similarly, Likewise, In the same way,
Contrast	but	while, although	In contrast, However, On the other hand, Conversely, Instead,
Refutation			On the contrary,
Concession	yet	although though even though it may appear that	Nevertheless, Even so, Admittedly, Despite this,
Emphasis			In fact, Actually,
Clarification			In other words, In simpler words, More simply,
Reason/Cause	for	because since	
Result	so	so so that	As a result, As a consequence, Consequently, Therefore, Thus,
Time Relationships		after as soon as before when while until whenever as	Afterward, First, Second, Next, Then, Finally, Subsequently, Meanwhile, In the meantime,
Condition		if even if unless provided that when	

Purpose	Coordinating Conjunctions (connect independent clauses)	Subordinating Conjunctions (begin dependent clauses)	Transitions (usually precede independent clauses)
Purpose		so that in order that	
Choice	or		
Conclusion			In conclusion, To summarize, As we have seen, In brief, In closing, To sum up, Finally,

Useful Vocabulary for Better Writing

Try these useful words and phrases as you write your essays. They can make your writing sound more academic, natural, and fluent.

Comparing

Words and Phrases	Examples
NOUN *is* COMPARATIVE ADJECTIVE *than* NOUN.	New York *is larger than* Rhode Island.
S + V + COMPARATIVE ADVERB *than* NOUN.	The cats ran *faster than* the dogs.
S + V. *In comparison*, S + V.	Canada has provinces. *In comparison,* Brazil has states.
Although NOUN *and* NOUN *are similar in* NOUN, …	*Although* France and Spain *are similar in* size, they are different in many ways.
Upon close inspection, S + V.	*Upon close inspection*, teachers in both schools discovered their students progressed *faster* when using games.
Compared to…	*Compared to* these roses, those roses last a long time.
NOUN *and* NOUN *are surprisingly similar.*	Brazil *and* the United States *are surprisingly similar.*
The same…	Brazil has states. *The same* can be said about Mexico.
Like NOUN, NOUN *also…*	*Like* Brazil, Mexico *also* has states.
Compared to…	*Compared to* U.S. history, Chinese history is complicated.
Both NOUN *and* NOUN…	*Both* dictatorships *and* oligarchies exemplify non-democratic ideologies.
Also, S + V. / *Likewise,* S + V.	The economies in South America seem to be thriving. *Likewise,* some Asian markets are doing very well these days.
Similarly, S + V. / *Similar to* S + V.	The economies in South America seem to be thriving. *Similarly,* some Asian markets are doing very well these days.

Contrasting

Words and Phrases	Examples
S + V. *In contrast,* S + V.	Algeria is a very large country. *In contrast,* the U.A.E. is very small.
Contrasted with / *In contrast to* NOUN	*In contrast to* soda, water is a better alternative.
Although / *Even though* / *Though…*	*Although* Spain and France are similar in size, they are different in many other ways.
Unlike NOUN, NOUN…	*Unlike* Spain, France borders eight countries.
However, S + V.	Canada has provinces. *However,* Brazil has states.
On the one hand, S + V. *On the other hand,* S + V.	*On the one hand,* Maggie loved to travel. *On the other hand,* she hated to be away from her home.
S + V, *yet* S + V.	People know that eating sweets is not good for their health, *yet* they continue to eat more sugar and fat than ever before.
NOUN *and* NOUN *are surprisingly different.*	Finland *and* Iceland *are surprisingly different.*

Telling a Story/Narrating

Words and Phrases	Examples
When I was NOUN / ADJ, *I would* VERB.	*When I was* a child, *I would* go fishing every weekend.
I had never felt so ADJ *in my life.*	*I had never felt so* anxious *in my life.*
I never would have thought that…	*I never would have thought that* I could win the competition.
Then the most amazing thing happened.	I thought my bag was gone forever. *Then the most amazing thing happened.*
Whenever I think back to that time, …	*Whenever I think back to* my childhood, I am moved by my grandparents' love for me.
I will never forget NOUN	*I will never forget* my wedding day.
I can still remember NOUN / *I will always remember* NOUN	*I can still remember* the day I started my first job.
NOUN *was the best / worst day of my life.*	The day I caught that fish *was the best day of my life.*
Every time S + V, S + V.	*Every time* I used that computer, I had a problem.
This was my first NOUN	*This was my first* time traveling alone.

Showing Cause and Effect

Words and Phrases	Examples
Because S + V / *Because of* S + V	*Because of* the traffic problems, it is easy to see why the city is building a new tunnel.
NOUN *can trigger* NOUN NOUN *can cause* NOUN	An earthquake *can trigger* tidal waves and *can cause* massive destruction.
Due to NOUN	*Due to* the economic sanctions, the unemployment rate skyrocketed.
On account of NOUN / *As a result of* NOUN / *Because of* NOUN	*On account of* the economic sanctions, the unemployment rate skyrocketed.
Therefore, NOUN / *As a result,* NOUN / *For this reason,* NOUN / *Consequently,* NOUN	Markets fell. *Therefore,* millions of people lost their life savings.
NOUN *will bring about* NOUN	The use of the Internet *will bring about a* change in education.
NOUN *has had a positive / negative effect on* NOUN	Computer technology *has had both positive and negative effects* on society.
The correlation… is clear / evident.	*The correlation* between junk food and obesity *is clear.*

Stating an Opinion

Words and Phrases	Examples
Without a doubt, doing NOUN *is* ADJECTIVE *idea / method / decision / way.*	*Without a doubt,* walking to work each day *is* an excellent *way* to lose weight.
Personally, I believe / think / feel / agree / disagree / suppose that NOUN	*Personally, I believe that* using electronic devices on a plane should be allowed.
Doing NOUN *should not be allowed.*	Texting in class *should not be allowed.*
In my opinion / view / experience, NOUN	*In my opinion,* talking on a cell phone in a movie theater is extremely rude.
For this reason, NOUN / *That is why I think* NOUN	*For this reason,* voters should not pass this law.

There are many benefits / advantages to NOUN.	There are many benefits to swimming every day.
There are many drawbacks / disadvantages to NOUN.	There are many drawbacks to eating meals at a restaurant.
I am convinced that S + V.	I am convinced that nuclear energy is safe and energy efficient.
NOUN should be required / mandatory.	Art education should be required of all high school students.
I prefer NOUN to NOUN.	I prefer rugby to football.
To me, banning / prohibiting NOUN makes sense.	To me, banning cell phones while driving makes perfect sense.
For all of these important reasons, S + V.	For all of these important reasons, cell phones in schools should be banned.
Based on NOUN, S + V.	Based on the facts presented, high-fat foods should be banned from the cafeteria.

Arguing and Persuading

Words and Phrases	Examples
It is important to remember S + V	It is important to remember that school uniforms would only be worn during school hours.
According to a recent survey, S + V	According to a recent survey, 85 percent of high school students felt they had too much homework.
Even more important, S + V	Even more important, statistics show the positive effects that school uniforms have on behavior.
Despite this, S + V	Despite this, many people remain opposed to school uniforms.
S must / should / ought to	Researchers must stop unethical animal testing.
For these reasons, S + V	For these reasons, public schools should require uniforms.
Obviously, S + V	Obviously, citizens will get used to this new law.
Without a doubt, S + V	Without a doubt, students ought to learn a foreign language.
I agree that S + V; however, S + V	I agree that a college degree is important; however, getting a practical technical license can also be very useful.

Giving a Counterargument

Words and Phrases	Examples
Proponents / Opponents may say S + V	Opponents of uniforms may say that students who wear uniforms cannot express their individuality.
On the surface this might seem logical / smart / correct; however, S + V	On the surface this might seem logical; however, it is not an affordable solution.
S + V; however, this is not the case.	The students could attend classes in the evening; however, this is not the case.
One could argue that S + V, but S + V	One could argue that working for a small company is very exciting, but it can also be more stressful than a job in a large company.
It would be wrong to say that S + V	It would be wrong to say that nuclear energy is 100 percent safe.
Some people believe that S + V	Some people believe that nuclear energy is the way of the future.

Upon further investigation, S + V	*Upon further investigation,* one begins to see problems with this line of thinking.
However, I cannot agree with this idea.	Some people think logging should be banned. *However, I cannot agree with this idea.*
Some people may say (one opinion), *but I* (opposite opinion.)	*Some people may say that* working from home is lonely, *but I* believe that working from home is easy, productive, and rewarding.
While NOUN *has its merits,* NOUN…	*While* working outside the home *has its merits,* working from home has many more benefits.
Although it is true that…, S + V	*Although it is true that* taking online classes can be convenient, it is difficult for many students to stay on task.

Reacting/Responding

Words and Phrases	Examples
TITLE *by* AUTHOR *is a / an …*	*Harry Potter and the Goblet of Fire by* J.K. Rowling *is an* entertaining book to read.
My first reaction to the prompt / news / article was / is NOUN	*My first reaction to the article was* fear.
When I read / look at / think about NOUN, *I was amazed / shocked / surprised …*	*When I read* the article, *I was surprised* to learn of his athletic ability.

NOTES

NOTES

NOTES

NOTES

NOTES

NOTES